The Rockwool Foundation Research Unit

Neighborhood Quality and Labor Market Outcomes: Evidence from Quasi-Random Neighborhood Assignment of Immigrants

Anna Piil Damm

University Press of Southern Denmark
Odense 2013

Neighborhood Quality and Labor Market Outcomes: Evidence from
Quasi-Random Neighborhood Assignment of Immigrants

Study Paper No. 47

Published by:
© The Rockwool Foundation Research Unit and
University Press of Southern Denmark

Copying from this book is permitted only within
institutions that have agreements with CopyDan,
and only in accordance with the limitations laid
down in the agreement

Address:
The Rockwool Foundation Research Unit
Sølvgade 10, 2nd floor
DK-1307 Copenhagen K

Telephone   +45 33 34 48 00

Fax   +45 33 34 48 99

E-mail   forskningsenheden@rff.dk

Home page   www.rff.dk

ISBN 978-87-90199-73-9
ISSN 0908-3979
February 2013
Print run: 300
Printed by: Specialtrykkeriet Viborg

Price: 60,00 DKK, including 25% VAT

Contents

I. Introduction 2

II Literature review 5

III. The importance of the social network for job finding 8
    III.A Data 8
    III.B Empirical model 11
    III.C Empirical results 13

IV. The causal effect of living in a socially deprived neighborhood
on individual labor market outcomes 15
    IV.A Data 15
    IV.B Danish spatial dispersal policy on refugees 19
    IV.C Instrumental variables model 24
    IV.D Ethnic stratification of networks 27

V. Conclusion 33

References 35

Tables and figures 38

Neighborhood Quality and Labor Market Outcomes: Evidence from Quasi-Random Neighborhood Assignment of Immigrants[1]

Anna Piil Damm[2]

February 2013

Using survey information about characteristics of personal contacts linked with administrative register information on employment status one year later, I show that unemployed survey respondents with many employed acquaintances have a higher job finding rate. Settlement in a socially deprived neighborhood may, therefore, hamper individual labor market outcomes because of lack of contact with employed individuals. I investigate this hypothesis by exploiting a unique natural experiment that occurred between 1986 and 1998 when refugee immigrants to Denmark were assigned to municipalities quasi-randomly, which successfully addresses the methodological problem of endogenous neighborhood selection. Taking account of location sorting, living in a socially deprived neighborhood does not affect labor market outcomes of refugee men. Furthermore, their labor market outcomes are not affected by the overall employment rate of men living in the neighborhood, but positively affected by the employment rate of non-Western immigrant men and co-national men living in the neighborhood. This is strong evidence that immigrants find jobs in part through their employed immigrant and co-ethnic contacts in the neighborhood of residence and that a high quality of contacts increases the individual's employment chances and annual earnings.

JEL codes: J60, J31, R30.
Keywords: Residential job search networks, referral, contacts, neighborhood quality, labor market outcomes.

---

[1] I have benefited from helpful comments and suggestions from Tor Eriksson, Nabanita Datta Gupta, Christian Dustmann, Jonathan Wadsworth, Giovanni Peri, Michael Rosholm, Peter Jensen, Astrid Würtz and participants at the II Workshop on Urban Economics 2012, the NORFACE Migration Conference "Migration: Economic Change, Social Change" 2011, the EEA/ESEM Conference 2011, the CReAM workshop, Sept. 2010, the Danish Microeconometric Network Workshop, Skagen 2010, the Aarhus University Immigration Workshop, Nov. 2010, the VATT seminar in Helsinki, May 2010, the ECON ASB Seminar, Dec. 2010 and the CIM workshop, Aug. 2008. This research was carried out in collaboration with the Rockwool Foundation Research Unit and the Danish National Centre for Social Research. I thank Margrethe L. Thuesen and Charlotte Duus for research assistance. The project was financed by a grant from the Strategic Research Program for Welfare Research for the project "Integration of ethnic minorities", grant 24-03-0288 from the Danish Research Agency and the NORFACE program on Migration.

[2] Department of Economics and Business, Aarhus University, Fuglesangs Allé 4, 8210 Aarhus V, Denmark. Tel: +45 87165146. Fax: +45 87165231. Email: apd@asb.dk.

I. Introduction

Widespread use of friends, relatives and acquaintances to search for jobs is a stylized fact (Rees, 1966; Granovetter, 1974, 1995; Holzer, 1988; Blau and Robins, 1990; Montgomery, 1991; Gregg and Wadsworth, 1996; Topa, 2001; Addison and Portugal, 2002; Wahba and Zenou, 2005; Bentolila, Michelacci and Suárez, 2010; Pellizari, 2010). Personal contacts may convey information about job vacancies and recommend friends, relatives and acquaintances with similar personal characteristics as themselves to their employer. For employers, job referrals lower the search costs as well as the screening costs of applicants.

But are all personal contacts equally useful for job referral? According to the strength-of-weak-ties theory by Granovetter (1973) weak ties, defined as acquaintances, are more useful for receipt of non-redundant information about job vacancies than strong ties, defined as friends and relatives. The more weak ties, the more non-redundant information about job openings will the individual receive. More recent social network theories, including Montgomery (1994) and Calvo-Armengól and Jackson (2004), instead argue that it is the quality, not the quantity, of personal contacts which is of key importance for job referral. The higher the quality of personal contacts, the more useful the contacts are for job referral.

An empirical analysis of whether weak ties and employed contacts are more productive in job search than strong ties and non-employed contacts requires self-reported information on characteristics of personal contacts. I have collected this information as part of a survey conducted in Denmark from Feb. to Nov. 2006 among a random sample of around 1,000 natives and random samples of around 1,000 immigrants from Turkey, Iran and Pakistan. In order to avoid reverse causality, i.e. that employment increases the number and quality of personal contacts, I limit my sample to unemployed survey respondents. For this sample, I estimate the effect of the quantity and quality of strong and weak ties on the individual's employment probability in Nov. 2006 or Nov. 2007, using information on the individual's employment status from administrative registers. For native and immigrant respondents alike, I find that respondents with a high employment rate of acquaintances are significantly more likely to find a job, after controlling for other personal characteristics and socio-economic characteristics of the municipality of residence. By contrast, having strong ties with a high employment rate and many acquaintances does not affect the individual's employment probability.

If geographic proximity facilitates information flows, network effects may operate in the neighborhood of residence. Therefore, living in a neighborhood with more unemployment may reduce the job chances. If so, concentration of unemployed workers in certain neighborhoods increases employment inequality in society.[3]

Results from studies using observational data are consistent with neighborhood job referral, i.e. that individuals who live in the same or adjacent neighborhoods sometimes refer each other to jobs.[4] By contrast, the quasi-experimental studies by Oreopoulos (2003) and Jacob (2004) find little role of neighborhood quality. Oreopoulos (2003) takes account of location sorting by exploiting quasi-random assignment of families to different residential housing projects in Toronto at the time at which their family reached the top of the waiting list. Jacob (2004) addresses location sorting by exploiting public housing demolitions in Chicago that forced families to leave high-rise public housing. Both studies convincingly solve the fundamental methodological challenge of self-selection into neighborhoods. However, their findings of a zero effect of neighborhood quality may be due to lack of variation in neighborhood quality.

I argue that the Danish Spatial Dispersal on Refugees which operated from 1986 until 1998 is an ideal quasi-experiment for investigation of whether living in a neighborhood with more unemployment is detrimental to individual labor market outcomes. At the time of receipt of asylum, placement officers working in the central office of the Danish Refugee Council assigned refugee families to housing in different locations in Denmark, exclusively on the basis of a questionnaire with personal information like household size. The placement officers did not meet face to face with refugees at the time of assignment. Since I observe all personal characteristics known to the placement officers in the administrative registers used for the analysis, I am able to condition on them in the regressions. As a consequence, characteristics of the neighborhood of assignment can be regarded as exogenous in the regressions.

---

[3] See e.g. Montgomery (1994).
[4] See e.g. Topa (2001), Weinberg, Reagan and Yankow (2004), Bayer, Ross and Topa (2008), Andersson, Burgess and Lane (2009) and Hellerstein, McInerney and Neumark (2011).

Moreover, recently neighborhood of residence data for Denmark was constructed by clustering all inhabited hectare cells into 2,296 neighborhoods, on average inhabited by 2,343 persons in 2004.[5] The approximately 15,400 refugee men subjected to the spatial dispersal policy were assigned to as many as 1,710 different neighborhoods located in 245 different municipalities[6] which gives me an extensive geographic variation in neighborhood characteristics. For instance, 16.7% of refugee men were quasi-randomly assigned to a socially deprived neighborhood defined as a neighborhood if the employment rate of the working-age population (18-60-year-olds) does not exceed 60%, while the remaining share was assigned to neighborhoods with less unemployment.[7] Moreover, since the spatial dispersal policy was carried out for more than a decade, I can include municipality of assignment fixed effects to control for unobserved, time-invariant municipality characteristics.

Six years after immigration as many as 35.2% of refugee men live in a socially deprived neighborhood. Controlling for personal characteristics, socio-economic characteristics of the municipality of residence and municipality fixed effects, they have a 4.5 percentage points lower employment probability and 10% lower real annual earnings than refugee men living in non-deprived neighborhoods. However, assignment to a socially deprived neighborhood has a zero effect on the employment probability and real annual earnings of refugee men 2-6 years after assignment. Using assignment to a socially deprived neighborhood as instrument for living in a socially deprived neighborhood 2-6 years after assignment, I find that a zero effect of current residence in a socially deprived neighborhood on individual labor market outcomes. I conclude that the worse labor market outcomes of immigrants who live in a socially deprived neighborhood are entirely due to negative self-selection of immigrants into socially deprived neighborhoods.

However, 74.7% of immigrant survey respondents who found their latest job through their social network found it through other immigrants. This suggests that non-Western

---

[5] In 2005, Anna P. Damm and Marie L. Schultz-Nielsen constructed neighborhoods for Denmark in collaboration with the Rockwool Research Unit. See Damm and Schultz-Nielsen (2008) for a description of the clustering process.

[6] In the observation period, Denmark was divided into 275 municipalities (local authorities), on average inhabited by 19,562 individuals (in 2004).

[7] In 2004, 4.1% of the overall population and 24% of non-Western immigrants in Denmark lived in a socially deprived neighborhood.

immigrants mainly have contact with neighbors of similar ethnic origin and limited contact with native neighbors. In that case, what matters is not the employment rate of the general population in the neighborhood, but the employment rate of immigrants of similar ethnic origin.[8] To test this hypothesis, I instrument the employment rate of non-Western immigrant (or co-national) men living in the current neighborhood of residence by the employment rate of non-Western immigrant (or co-national) men living in the neighborhood of assignment in the year of assignment. I find that a percentage point increase (around the mean) in the employment rate of non-Western immigrant men aged 18-60 living in the neighborhood of residence 2-6 years after immigration increases the individual's employment probability by 0.2 percentage points and real annual earnings by 2%. In addition, I find that one percentage point increase in the employment rate of co-national men aged 18-60 living in the neighborhood of residence 2-6 years after immigration (around the mean) increases real annual earnings by 2%. These results are robust to controlling for the quantity of non-Western immigrant (co-national) men living in the neighborhood of residence.

The next section gives a brief literature review. Section III presents survey evidence on job search channels in Denmark and investigates whether and how the social network promotes individual employment. Section IV describes the Danish Spatial Dispersal Policy on Refugees and exploits it to provide quasi-experimental evidence on whether settlement in a neighborhood with more unemployment hampers individual labor market outcomes. Section V offers conclusions.

II. Literature review

Social network theories emphasize the importance of different characteristics of the social network for job referral, e.g. strong versus weak ties and the quality versus the quantity of contacts.

According to the strength-of-weak-ties theory by Granovetter (1973), the degree of overlap of two individuals' friendship networks varies directly with the strength of their tie to one another. If the two individuals are acquaintances (rather than close friends), there is little overlap in their networks. Such weak ties are more likely to convey non-

---

[8] This intuition is consistent with the theoretical model by Calvó-Armengol and Jackson (2004).

redundant information about job vacancies and therefore more useful for obtaining a job than strong ties, defined as family and close friends.

The quasi-experimental papers on the effect of living in an ethnic enclave on immigrant labor market outcomes by Edin, Fredriksson and Åslund (2003) and Damm (2009) emphasize the importance of having many weak ties. Edin et al. (2003) exploit a Swedish Spatial Dispersal Policy on refugees to estimate the earnings effect of the number of co-nationals living in the municipality of residence 8 years after immigration. As instrument they use the number of co-nationals in the municipality of assignment and municipality of assignment fixed effects are included to control for time-invariant municipality characteristics. They find a positive earnings effect of the number of co-nationals living in the municipality of residence for low-skilled refugees, while the effect is insignificant for highly skilled refugees. Using the Danish Spatial Dispersal Policy on refugees in place from 1986 until 1998, Damm (2009) finds a positive effect of the number of co-nationals living in the municipality of residence 7 years after immigration on individual real annual earnings, for both low- and highly skilled refugees. As instrument Damm (2009) uses the number of co-nationals assigned together with individual i to municipality j. A likely explanation is that co-ethnic contacts convey valuable information about better-paying jobs.

More recent social network theories by Montgomery (1994) and Calvó-Armengol and Jackson (2004) argue that the quality of contacts matter for job referral. Montgomery (1994) models the impact of social interaction on employment transitions and inequality in a way that links the notion of strong versus weak ties to the social structure. In his model, society is composed of many two-person groups. Each individual may be employed or not. Unemployed individuals find jobs through strong ties (intra-group interaction), weak ties (random intergroup interaction) and formal channels. Furthermore, the model assumes that social interactions are characterized by inbreeding bias, making the employment status of one's strong tie critical. Montgomery uses his model to show that an increase in weak-tie interactions reduces employment inequality. Moreover, an increase in weak-tie interactions increases the steady-state employment rate if inbreeding by employment status among weak ties is sufficiently low.

Calvó-Armengol and Jackson (2004) explore the implications of exogenous information networks by setting up a model where agents obtain information about job opportunities through an explicitly modeled network of social contacts. They show that employment is positively correlated across time and agents. Moreover, they examine inequality. If staying in the labor market is costly and one group (e.g. blacks versus whites) starts with a worse employment status, then that group's drop-out rate will be higher and their employment prospects will be persistently below that of the other group.

The empirical study by Munshi (2003) provides convincing evidence that, besides the number of contacts, the quality of contacts is also important. Munshi (2003) studies the effect of the size and vintage of the origin-community based networks of Mexican immigrants in the US on their employment probability and occupation category (agriculture or not). Using the amount of rainfall in the origin-community as an instrument for the size of the network in the destination and including individual fixed effects in the regressions to control for selective emigration, Munshi (2003) finds that the larger the *established* network is, the more likely the same individual is to be employed and hold a higher paying non-agricultural job.

If geographic proximity facilitates information flows, network effects may operate in the neighborhood of residence. Previous empirical papers find contrasting evidence on whether the individuals who live in the same or adjacent neighborhoods refer each other to jobs.

Using census tracts in Chicago, Topa (2001) estimates a structural model that explicitly incorporates local interactions. His model estimates show that high unemployment in one tract is associated with more unemployment in neighboring tracts that can be explained by the characteristics of the neighboring tracts alone. He interprets this as evidence of local spillover effects. Similarly, Andersson et al. (2009) find empirical evidence that immigrants living in census tracts with large numbers of employed neighbors are more likely to have jobs than immigrants in areas with fewer employed neighbors. Moreover, Bayer et al. (2008) show that people who live in the same census block tend to work together. They interpret this as evidence of neighborhood job referrals. Using a confidential version of NLSY79, Weinberg et al. (2004) estimate large effects of neighborhood social characteristics on labor market activity after exploiting the panel aspects of their data and provide evidence of non-linear neighborhood effects: social influences have the greatest proportional effects in the worst neighborhoods.

In contrast, the only quasi-experimental neighborhood effects studies to date, Oreopoulos (2003) and Jacob (2004), find little role of the neighborhood quality on individual achievement. Oreopoulos (2003) investigates whether neighborhood quality affects long-term labor market outcomes of individuals who were assigned as children to different residential housing projects in Toronto at the time at which their family reached the top of the waiting list. Assignment was based mainly on household size and families were unable to specify project preferences. Jacob (2004) argues that the public housing demolition in Chicago can be regarded as a natural experiment which enables estimation of the intent-to-treat effect of public housing demolitions in Chicago and the average treatment effect of living in public housing on student achievement. Jacob (2004) show that the majority of households that leave high-rise public housing due to the demolitions move to neighborhoods that are similar to those they left. Therefore, his finding of a zero effect of neighborhood quality can be explained by lack of neighborhood quality variation.

For an extensive summary of the economic literature on job information networks and neighborhood effects, see Ioannides and Loury (2004).

III. The importance of the social network for job finding

III.A Data

The primary data source is the Welfare Research Survey data collected by SFI Survey in Feb.-Nov. 2006 in Denmark for a random sample of roughly 4,000 18-45-year-old individuals - around 1,000 natives and 1,000 immigrants (i.e. foreign born individuals whose parents are also foreign born or have foreign citizenship) from each of the following countries: Turkey, Iran or Pakistan.[9] The overall response rate was 60%.[10] The

---

[9] Immigration from Turkey and Pakistan began in the late 1960s and the early 1970s with immigration of unskilled men ("guest workers") who found employment in the Danish manufacturing industry. Many guest workers subsequently brought their families to Denmark and many of their children have found their spouse in the country of origin and brought them to Denmark. Immigration from Iran began in the mid

Welfare Research Survey is a cross-sectional micro data set for 2006. The data collection process consisted of telephone interviews supplemented by face-to-face interviews. If possible, the interview was conducted in Danish and otherwise in Turkish, Farsi or Urdu. Therefore, insufficient host-country language skills were not a barrier for participation. Using a unique person identifier, I link the Welfare Research Survey with administrative register information from Statistics Denmark on the individual's demographic characteristics and educational attainment in 2006, employment status in Nov. 2006 and Nov. 2007 as well as information on work experience from 1980 until 2004 (measured in number of years of full-time work).[11] In addition, I add socio-economic characteristics of the individual's municipality of residence in 2006 to the Welfare Research Survey. The information on municipality characteristics has been constructed from the administrative registers by Statistics Denmark. Table 1.A summarizes the personal attributes and the municipality of residence characteristics of survey respondents separately for natives (column 1) and immigrants (column 2). Survey respondents are on average 33.5 years old. While immigrant and native respondents are similar in terms of age, immigrant survey respondents are significantly more likely to be married, are significantly less likely to have completed more than nine years of education, have significantly fewer years of work experience in Denmark and are significantly less likely to be employed in Nov. 2006 or Nov. 2007.

In the Welfare Research Survey labor force participants were asked about their means of finding their latest (employee) job. Table 2 summarizes the results. As reported in Panel A of Table 2 (columns 1-2), the majority of natives (71%) and immigrants (67%) had found their latest job by means of direct job search. The most common direct job search channel was "direct application to the employer"; that channel was used by 44% of the respondents who found their latest job through direct search (see Panel B of Table

---

1980s, when a large number of asylum seekers received a residence permit in Denmark. (Mogensen and Mathiessen 2002).

[10] Deding, Fridberg and Jakobsen (2008) have carefully examined determinants of non-response in the survey by linking the survey with administrative registers. The findings are that immigrants from Pakistan were especially difficult to contact, while refusals were high among Turkish immigrants. Moreover, they conclude that individuals aged 18-29, individuals with children and women were significantly easier to contact, while highly educated and employed individuals were more likely to cooperate.

[11] The Rockwool Research Unit has granted me access to their administrative register information from Statistics Denmark.

2, columns 1-2). However, a substantial share of respondents had found their latest job by means of informal job search, i.e. through the social network (relatives, close friends or acquaintances): 16.6% of natives and 26.3% of immigrants survey respondents. These findings are in line with two previous Danish surveys which were conducted by the Rockwool Research Unit in 1996 for the general population and in 1998-1999 for the immigrant population. According to these two surveys, 19% of native workers and 23% of immigrant workers had found their current job through friends, relatives or other acquaintances or the union (Mogensen and Mathiessen, 2000). Compared to evidence for most other European countries and the U.S., the share of workers in Denmark who has found the latest job through the social network is rather low. A possible explanation may well be that formal job search channels are relatively efficient in Denmark, as argued by Pellazari (2010). Furthermore, division of immigrant respondents into low- and highly skilled (defined as having completed at least nine years of school) shows that a higher share of low-skilled immigrants have found the latest job through their social network: 36% as opposed to 23.3% of highly skilled (see columns 3-4 in Table 2).

I have obtained information about the quality of the social network by asking the following survey questions which I use as measures of the usefulness of the social network for job referral. First: "Do few or many of your i) family members in Denmark, ii) close friends in Denmark and iii) other adult contacts have a job?" Second: "Which level of education does most of your i) family members in Denmark, ii) close friends in Denmark and iii) other adult contacts have?" If at least 50% of members of a given social network category are employed, the indicator for having a social network with a high employment rate takes the value 1, 0 otherwise. Similarly, if at least 50% of members of a given social network category have either vocational secondary education or tertiary education, the indicator for having a highly educated (i.e. skilled) social network takes the value 1, 0 otherwise.

I construct variables for the individual's work attitude and the work attitude of strong ties (family and close friends in Denmark) from the answers to the following survey questions: First: "To which extent do i) you, ii) most of your family members in Denmark and iii) most of your close friends in Denmark agree with the statement that unemployed individuals ought to be willing to move in order to get a permanent job?" Second: "To which extent do i) you, ii) most of your family members in Denmark and iii) close friends in Denmark agree with the statement that unemployed individuals ought to be willing to take a job at a salary below the income as unemployed?" Third: "to which extent do i) you, ii) most of your family members in Denmark and iii) close friends in Denmark agree with the statement that it is humiliating to receive social assistance?"

Columns 1 and 2 in Table 1.B summarize the self-reported individual characteristics including social network characteristics for native and immigrant survey respondents, respectively. Significant mean differences exist in self-reported social network characteristics between native and immigrant respondents. At the time of the interview, natives had a higher employment rate than immigrants. On average natives have more acquaintances in the host-country than immigrants and a larger share of natives has a social network with a high employment rate and high level of education than immigrants. This may be evidence that job seekers with many acquaintances and a social network with a high employment rate and high level of education increase the chances of getting a job. Alternatively, it may reflect reverse causality, i.e. employed individuals get more acquaintances and more employed acquaintances through their job, and that friendships tend to form within skill groups. The two groups of respondents also differ significantly when it comes to work attitudes. Turning to work attitudes of the respondents, a larger share of immigrant respondents than Danish respondents agree with the views that i) "I primarily work to earn a living" and ii) "unemployed individuals should be willing to move to get a permanent job", iii) "Unemployed individuals ought to be willing to work at a salary below the income as unemployed" and iv) "it is humiliating to receive social assistance". Agreeing with these statements may be interpreted as evidence of a strong work ethic. If so, the immigrant respondents on average have a stronger work ethic than Danish respondents. However, a smaller share of immigrant than native respondents has family in Denmark who agrees with the above-mentioned views ii)-iii), suggesting that the work ethic of family of immigrant respondents is weaker than that of Danish respondents.

III.B Empirical model

In order to avoid reverse causality (i.e. that having a job may increase the size and improve the quality of your social network), I limit my sample to survey respondents who did not have a job in the week before the interview (conducted from Feb. to Nov. 2006) but was looking for one, henceforth referred to as the sample of unemployed respondents. The Danish labor market was extremely tight in 2006; the (net) unemployment rate in full-time equivalents was 3.9% (www.statistikbanken.dk/AULAAR). Therefore, only 69 native survey respondents and 239 survey respondents of immigrant origin were unemployed in the week before the interview. The dependent variable is an indicator for being employed in Nov. 2006 or Nov. 2007 according to the administrative registers. Among unemployed survey respondents 65% of natives sand 49% of immigrants were employed in Nov. 2006 or Nov. 2007, which means that they have found a job shortly after the interview.

I investigate the importance of characteristics of the individual's social network on job finding for the sample of unemployed respondents in the following way. First, I evaluate how much inclusion of social network explanatory variables increases the explanatory power of the standard model with personal and area of residence attributes as employment determinants. Henceforth, I refer to the extended employment model as the social network model. Second, I use the estimated social network model to find out which, if any, social network characteristics have a significant effect on the individual's employment probability. The social network model is given by

(1)
$$y_{ij} = W_i \delta + X_i \beta + V_j \gamma + \varepsilon_{ij}$$

where subscript i denotes the individual and subscript j denotes the municipality of residence. The dependent variable y takes the value 1 if individual i is employed in Nov. 2006 or Nov. 2007, 0 otherwise. W is the set of self-reported social network characteristics. The standard set of explanatory variables is X: personal attributes and V: socioeconomic characteristics of the municipality of residence. ε is the error term. Values of explanatory variables refer to 2006.

W contains variables describing i) the size of the individual's social network, ii) the quality of strong (family and close friends in Denmark) and weak ties (other contacts in Denmark, henceforth referred to as acquaintances in Denmark), iii) predominant contact to other immigrants, iv) the individual's own work ethic and v) the work ethic of family in Denmark.

For natives, X consists of indicators for sex, marital status, having a child aged 0-2, having a child aged 3-17, educational attainment (0-9 years, 10-12 years, 13 years or more) and being proficient in English, work experience, work experience squared and interactions between gender and indicators for i) marital status, ii) having a child aged 0-2 and iii) having a child aged 3-17. For immigrants, X contains in addition age, age squared and indicators for being proficient in Danish, year of immigration, country of origin and reason for immigration. V contains three variables: log number of inhabitants, log average annual gross income and the unemployment rate in the municipality of residence.

Columns 3 and 4 of Table 1 show the summary statistics for the sample of unemployed respondents separately for natives and immigrants.

III.C Empirical results

Table 3 reports the estimation results of the standard employment model for unemployed survey respondents separately for natives (first column) and immigrants (fifth column). The standard employment model explains, respectively, 0.213 and 0.29 of the total variation in employment status in Nov. 2006/2007. For immigrants, Danish and English language proficiency are, respectively, associated with 17 percentage points (or 35%) and 29 percentage points (or 59%) higher employment probability. However, these estimates are likely to be upward biased due to omitted variables like innate abilities.

Next, I include self-reported social network characteristics and own work attitude as additional explanatory variables. I use three different specifications of the social network model for natives and four different specifications for immigrants. The first specification includes two types of social network characteristics as explanatory variables: i) the number of acquaintances (standardized to have zero mean and a standard deviation of 1), ii) the quality of strong and weak ties (indicators for having family, close friends and acquaintances in Denmark of which the majority are highly educated and employed). The second specification also includes the interaction between the number of acquaintances and an indicator for having acquaintances of which the majority are employed. The third specification for immigrants includes in addition to the first specification an indicator for having predominant contact to other immigrants and the interaction between the number of acquaintances and the indicator for having predominant contact to other immigrants.

The final specification for both natives and immigrants includes, in addition to the second-to-last specification for the respective group, explanatory variables describing i) the individual's own work ethic and ii) the work ethic of family in Denmark.[12]

The estimation results of the different specifications of the social network model are also reported in Table 3 (columns 2-4 for natives, columns 6-9 for immigrants). Inclusion of social network characteristics which measure the size and quality of the individual's social network increases the explained part of the variance from 0.213 to 0.300 for natives and from 0.290 to 0.336 for immigrants. Additional inclusion of work ethic variables increases the explanatory power of the model from 0.300 to 0.400 for natives and from 0.319 to 0.358 for immigrants.

For natives and immigrants alike and in all specifications, the number of acquaintances has an insignificant effect on the individual's employment probability, while having acquaintances of which the majority are employed promotes employment. Having acquaintances of which the majority is employed is associated with 49 percentage points (or 75%) and 12 percentage points (or 24%) higher employment probability for natives and immigrants, respectively. However, these estimates are likely to be upward biased due to omitted variables like innate abilities. The quality of strong ties (family and close friends) has an insignificant effect on the individual's employment probability.[13] For immigrants, I also find that having primarily immigrant acquaintances is associated with 13 percentage points (or 27%) lower employment probability. However, note that the estimate may be biased due to lack of control for unobserved individual abilities and read Section IV.D for an estimate of the causal effect of exposure to non-Western immigrants living in the neighborhood on labor market outcomes of non-Western immigrant men.

For natives and immigrants alike, the work ethic of family in Denmark does not influence the individual's employment probability. Similarly, with one exception, all

---

[12] Measures of the work ethic of close friends in Denmark are excluded from the set of explanatory variables because of a high correlation between the work ethic of family in Denmark and of close friends in Denmark.

[13] The exception is that immigrants with family members in Denmark of which at least half are employed have a significantly lower employment probability (at the ten percent significance level). However, this counter-intuitive result is driven by female respondents; the estimate turns insignificant after inclusion of the interaction between an indicator for woman and the indicator for having family members in Denmark of which at least half are employed.

measures of own work ethic have an insignificant effect on the individual's employment probability.[14] This suggests that either work attitudes have little influence on the individuals' employment probability, or the self-reported work attitudes are not reliable measures.

Summing up, estimation results for the social network model reported in Table 3 show that one social network characteristic is important for job finding of natives and immigrants alike: having acquaintances of which the majority is employed. If individuals are sometimes referred to vacant jobs through contacts in their neighborhood, this finding suggests that residents in socially deprived neighborhoods (i.e. neighborhoods with a high concentration of jobless individuals) may have a lower employment probability than residents outside socially deprived neighborhoods, in part because they have fewer employed contacts in the neighborhood. I now turn to empirical investigation of this hypothesis.

IV. The causal effect of living in a socially deprived neighborhood on individual labor market outcomes

This section exploits a quasi-experiment to investigate empirically whether residence in a socially deprived neighborhood hampers individual labor market outcomes or whether the adverse labor market outcomes of residents in socially deprived neighborhoods are entirely due to negative self-selection of individuals into these neighborhoods.

IV.A Data

I link two primary data sources using a unique person identifier: i) administrative register data from Statistics Denmark 1986-2004 and ii) neighborhood of residence information from the Rockwool Foundation Research Unit for the entire population in Denmark 1985-2004. The neighborhoods are constructed on basis of geo-referenced data provided by the National Square Grid – Denmark. The 431,233 inhabited hectare cells in Denmark are clustered into 2,296 neighborhoods, on average inhabited by 2,343 persons in 2004. The neighborhoods are homogenous in terms of population size and housing type and

---

[14] The exception is that natives who agree with the view that "unemployed individuals should be willing to move to get a permanent job" have a lower employment probability – in contrast to what one would expect.

delineated by physical barriers (like major roads, lakes and forests) (Damm and Schultz-Nielsen, 2008).

Previous Danish studies have defined a socially deprived neighborhood as a neighborhood in which more than 40% of the working-age population receive public income transfers or the non-Western immigrant share exceeds 30% (Andersen, 2005; Damm, Schultz-Nielsen and Tranæs, 2006). Using this definition, 90 out of 2,296 neighborhoods were socially deprived in 2004. Damm et al. (2006) show that the mean gross income is relatively low and the share of inhabitants who have committed a crime is relatively high in socially deprived neighborhoods. However, social network theory argues that what matters for individual labor market outcomes is whether or not a neighbor is employed and not whether or not the neighbor receives public income transfers. Therefore, I define a neighborhood as socially deprived if the employment rate in the working-age population (ages 18-60) does not exceed 60%. This definition is equivalent to defining a socially deprived neighborhood as a neighborhood in which the jobless share of the working age population exceeds 40%. According to my definition, 119 out of 2,296 neighborhoods were socially deprived in 2004.[15] 4.1% of the overall population in Denmark lived in a socially deprived neighborhood in 2004. By contrast, 24% of non-Western immigrants lived in a socially deprived neighborhood. Note also that in Nov. 2004, only 60% of non-Western immigrants in Denmark were employed while 82.8% of the overall population were employed.

Ideally, estimation of the causal effect of living in a socially deprived neighborhood on individual labor market outcomes requires random assignment of individuals to the two types of neighborhoods, socially deprived and non-deprived. Below I argue that such an experiment has been undertaken for newly recognized refugees who were subject to the ordinary Spatial Dispersal Policy on Refugees in Denmark in the period 1986-1998. Therefore, for this part of the analysis I extract a longitudinal panel of all male non-Western immigrants aged 18-59 who immigrated in the period 1986-1998 from one of the eight largest refugee-sending countries (Lebanon, Iraq, Iran, Sri Lanka, Somalia,

---

[15] Defining in addition a neighborhood as socially deprived if the non-Western immigrant share exceeds 30% would not add any neighborhoods to the set of socially deprived neighborhoods in the period 1986-1996, i.e. the period in which newly recognized refugees were subject to the Danish Spatial Dispersal Policy. They are already defined as socially deprived according to my definition.

Vietnam, Afghanistan and Ethiopia).[16] Refugees from these countries constitute more than 86% of the total number of permanent residence permits granted to refugees between 1985 and 1997.[17] I exclude family-reunified immigrants by excluding individuals if i) they were married to an individual from a non-refugee-sending country or ii) immigrated more than a year later than the spouse. These selection criteria result in a balanced sample of 15,436 male refugees who are observed annually until six years after immigration.

Using a unique personal identifier, I link the information about the neighborhood of assignment (defined as the neighborhood of residence in the year of immigration) with the longitudinal panel of male refugees. Moreover, I link the longitudinal panel of male refugees with socio-economic characteristics of the municipality of assignment (defined as the municipality of residence in the year of immigration). Summary statistics (initial values) of the balanced sample of male refugees are shown in appendix Table A1.

Six years after immigration 35.2% of male refugees live in a socially deprived neighborhood; their employment rate is only 24.8% while 33.8% of refugee men living in a non-deprived neighborhood are employed. This difference may simply reflect observed differences in personal and area characteristics. To investigate whether this is the case, I estimate

(2)

$$y_{ijk(t+6)} = \alpha D_{ijk(t+6)} + X_{it}\beta + V_{j^*}\gamma + \delta_k + \delta_t + \delta_{j^*} + \varepsilon_{ijk(t+6)}$$

where the subscripts denote i: individual, j: municipality of residence, k: country of origin, t: year of assignment (i.e. year of immigration), j^*: municipality of assignment. The dependent variable y is either a dummy variable for individual i living in municipality j in year $t+6$ being employed in year $t+6$ or the individual's log real annual earnings in year $t+6$. The key explanatory variable is a dummy D which takes the value 1

---

[16] Refugees from Former Yugoslavia are excluded from my sample because – in contrast to refugees from other refugee-sending countries – they were initially granted provisional asylum and were therefore subject to a special dispersal policy of refugees implemented in 1993 (called the Bosnian program). Refugees subject to the Bosnian program were accommodated in refugee-reception centres and so-called refugee villages.

[17] For these groups, the number of non-refugee immigrants relative to the total number of immigrants (after exclusion of immigrants who were married to a resident in Denmark from a non-refugee sending country in the year of immigration) is less than 4.8%.

if individual *i* lived in a socially deprived neighborhood in municipality *j* in year *t+6*, 0 otherwise. Control variables are *X*: personal attributes in year *t* (age and age squared and indicators for marital status, having a young child, having an old child and educational attainment), *V*: socio-economic and demographic characteristics of the municipality of assignment (log number of inhabitants, log average gross income, the unemployment rate, log percentage of non-Western immigrants, and log percentage of co-nationals) and δ: fixed effects for country of origin, year of assignment and – in specification 2 – also for municipality of assignment. ε is the error term.

Using the two different specifications, the estimated correlations between living in a socially deprived neighborhood six years after immigration and individual labor market outcomes six years after immigration for the overall sample are reported in Table 4 (columns 1-2: employment model, columns 7-8: earnings model). Refugees who live in a socially deprived neighborhood six years after immigration have a 4.5 pct. points lower employment rate and 9.5-10.1 percent lower real annual earnings than refugees who live elsewhere, after controlling for initial values of personal attributes, socioeconomic and demographic characteristics of the municipality of assignment in the year of immigration, year of immigration, country of origin, and – in specification 2 also - municipality of assignment. Furthermore, I investigate whether refugees who live in a socially deprived neighborhood six years after immigration have worse labor market outcomes irrespective of skill level by estimating equation 2 separately for low- and highly skilled (i.e. at least 10 years of schooling) men. These coefficient estimates are also reported in Table 4 (columns 3-6: employment model, columns 9-12: earnings model). Living in a socially deprived neighborhood six years after immigration is associated with a significantly lower employment probability for both skill groups and, for highly skilled refugees only, also with significantly lower real annual earnings.

I will use instrumental variable techniques in order to test whether the negative statistical association between residence in a socially deprived neighborhood and individual labor market outcomes is a causal effect. In particular, I will instrument the indicator for current residence in a socially deprived neighborhood by an indicator for having been assigned to a socially deprived neighborhood as part of the Ordinary Spatial Dispersal Policy on Refugees. This instrument is valid if refugees subject to the Ordinary

Spatial Dispersal Policy were randomly distributed across neighborhoods or, if at least, I can control for all personal attributes which affected the assignment to neighborhood type. Moreover, the instrument is a strong predictor if a substantial share of refugees remains in the neighborhood of assignment for some years. I now turn to a short description of the Ordinary Spatial Dispersal Policy on Refugees.

IV.B Danish spatial dispersal policy on refugees

In 1986, the Danish Government, through the Danish Refugee Council (henceforth referred to as "the Council"), implemented a two-stage dispersal policy for asylum seekers who had their applications approved, i.e. refugees.[18] The main objective was to disperse refugees across counties and municipalities according to the number of existing inhabitants.[19] In a first step, the Council allocated refugees proportional to the number of inhabitants to counties; in a second step, and within counties, refugees were proportionally allocated to the number of inhabitants to municipalities (Danish Refugee Council, CIU, 1996, p. 8-9). This policy was in place until the end of 1998. Over this thirteen-year period, 76,673 individuals were granted refugee status (Statistical Yearbook 1992, Table 60; Statistical Yearbook 1997, Table 68; Statistical Yearbook 2000, Table 55) and were allocated across municipalities by the Council.

Before approval of refugee status, asylum seekers lived in Red Cross Reception Centers spread across Denmark. About ten days after receipt of asylum, those who were granted refugee status were assigned to temporary housing in one of Denmark's 15 counties by the central Council office (Danish Refugee Council, CIU, 1996, p. 9). After settlement in the assigned county, the local office of the Council assisted assigned refugees in finding permanent housing in one of the municipalities within the county.

At receipt of asylum, refugees needed to fill in a questionnaire, which was available to the Council when making the allocation decision. The questionnaire asked refugees to provide a few personal details: birth date, marital status, number of children, nationality, and language. Placement officers in the central Council office did not meet the refugees

---

[18] Until June 2002, Denmark gave asylum to individuals who were defined as refugees according to the Geneva Convention and to individuals who would not qualify as refugees under the Convention, but who for other reasons should not be required to return to the home country ('de facto' refugees - see Coleman and Wadensjö, 1999, for details).
[19] Following the convention, I refer to a person who seeks asylum as an "asylum seeker", and to a person whose asylum status has been approved as a "refugee".

in person; dispersal decisions were made exclusively on the basis of the questionnaire information. For instance, the information about household composition was used to determine whether to search for housing for a single individual or a family. Hence, the Council's allocation may have been influenced by some of the information in the questionnaire, like family size. I observe all these characteristics in the analysis, and condition on them. By contrast, the Council's allocation was not influenced by educational attainment or family income since the questionnaire did not ask about such personal details.

Note that the Council did not consider individual location wishes in the assignment process. However, a small fraction of refugees refused the offer of permanent housing in the location of assignment in which case the Council reassigned them to another location. I define the neighborhood of assignment as the initial neighborhood of residence observed in the administrative registers, i.e. the neighborhoods of residence at the time of receipt of asylum. Re-assignment is only a minor concern for the instrumental variables analysis because, in the rare case of re-assignment, it typically took place after the initial move to the location of assignment, in which case the location of assignment is observed in the administrative registers.

After settlement in the location of assignment, refugees participated in Danish language courses during an introductory period of 18 months while receiving social assistance. Although individuals were urged to stay in the assigned municipality during the entire introductory period, there were no relocation restrictions. Individuals could move away from the municipality of assignment at any time, if they could find alternative housing elsewhere. Receipt of social benefits was unconditional on residing in the municipality of assignment.

The spatial dispersal policy was successful. Refugees who got asylum in the period 1980-1984 primarily settled in one of the large cities (Copenhagen, Aarhus, Odense and Aalborg) (see Figure 1). By contrast, refugees who got asylum in the period 1986-1998 were fairly evenly distributed across municipalities relative to the local population size as shown in Figure 2. Moreover, the Council's Annual Report (Danish Refugee Council, 1987, p. 30-31) shows that only two years after the introduction of the dispersal policy refugees lived in 243 out of the 275 municipalities.

Table 5 shows that the dispersal policy had a very visible effect on the settlement pattern across neighborhood type (socially deprived or non-deprived) of refugees. It shows the geographical distribution across neighborhood type of the overall population in Denmark and non-Western immigrants in 1991 and individuals in the balanced sample of refugee men. The non-Western immigrant population was heavily overrepresented in socially deprived neighborhoods in 1991. 22.8% of non-Western immigrants lived in such a neighborhood as compared to 3.9% of the overall population in Denmark. By contrast, as a consequence of the spatial dispersal policy on refugees, only 16.7% of individuals in the balanced sample of refugee men subject to the Ordinary Spatial Dispersal Policy on Refugees initially lived in a socially deprived neighborhood. Refugees were initially renters. However, as shown in appendix Table A1, refugee men assigned to a socially deprived neighborhood were initially overrepresented in large apartment blocks (88% vs. 42%) and public housing units (81% vs. 23%).

Next, I divide the individuals in the balanced sample of refugee men into two groups: 1) individuals assigned to (i.e. initially live in) a socially deprived neighborhood (2,573 individuals, i.e. 16.7%) and 2) individuals assigned elsewhere (12,863 individuals). One can consider assignment to a socially deprived neighborhood by the authorities as a treatment and refer to the group of individuals who received treatment as the treatment group. Individuals who were assigned to a non-deprived neighborhood constitute the control group. Individuals in the treatment group are assigned in the period 1986-1998 to one of 166 socially deprived neighborhoods (many of which are adjacent). These socially deprived neighborhoods are located in the four Danish cities (Copenhagen, Aarhus, Odense and Aalborg) and 34 towns in Denmark[20] and include immigrant-dense residential areas which are often mentioned in the Danish media because of incidents of e.g. vandalism.[21] Maps of the socially deprived neighborhoods in the four largest

---

[20] Helsingoer, Kokkedal, Hilleroed, Kgs. Lyngby, Herlev, Albertslund, Hvidovre, Broendby, Ishoej, Hoeje Taastrup, Hedehusene, Roskilde, Holbaek, Kalundborg, Korsoer, Slagelse, Naestved, Nakskov, Svendborg, Soenderborg, Haderslev, Esbjerg, Kolding, Fredericia, Vejle, Horsens, Silkeborg, Randers, Viborg, Holstebro, Nykoebing Mors, Thisted, Frederikshavn and Hjoerring.

[21] My definition of socially deprived neighborhoods includes Tingbjerg and Lundtoftegade in Copenhagen, Taastrupgård, Vejleaaparken and Broendby Strand in the suburbs west of Copenhagen, Vollsmose in Odense, Byparken in Svendborg, Varbergparken in Haderslev, Kvaglund and Stengaardsvej in Esbjerg, Sundparken and Soenderbro in Horsens, Skovvejen/Skovparken in Kolding, Gellerupparken and Bispehaven in Aarhus and Sebbersundvej in Aalborg.

municipalities are shown in appendix Figures A1-A4. Each neighborhood consists of a number of hectare cells. Hectare cells marked with red are located in socially deprived neighborhoods while hectare cells marked with blue are located in non-deprived neighborhoods. In the analysis below neighborhoods are used as the spatial unit.

The implementation of the spatial dispersal policy gives no reason to believe that the allocation of refugees across neighborhoods has been in response to individual abilities. This is apparent from Table 6, where I report the mean values of personal attributes at the time of immigration of the treatment and control groups (columns 1 and 2) and a t-test of difference in means (third column). The t-test of difference in means shows that there are no significant differences in educational attainment between the two groups. Older, married individuals with children aged 3-17 were initially over-represented in socially deprived neighborhoods, because large apartments suitable for families are overrepresented in socially deprived neighborhoods. Furthermore, column 1 of appendix Table A2 shows the coefficient estimates from linear regression of an indicator for assignment to a socially deprived neighborhood on personal attributes at the time of assignment (age, indicators for educational attainment, being married, having a child aged 0-2, having a child aged 3-17, year of immigration and country of origin). The R^2-value is very low (0.035) and the only significant coefficient estimates are: the indicator for having a child aged 3-17, year of immigration (refugees who immigrated at the end of the period were more likely to be assigned to a socially deprived neighborhood) and country of origin (relative to Iranian refugees, refugees from Vietnam were slightly more likely to be assigned to a socially deprived neighborhood, while refugees from Sri Lanka were slightly less likely to be assigned to a socially deprived neighborhood). This suggests that conditional on a few observed personal attributes (having a child aged 3-17, year of immigration and country of origin), refugees have initially been randomly allocated across neighborhood type (socially deprived or not).

Moreover, I regress other demographic and socio-economic characteristics of the neighborhood of assignment in the year of assignment on individual characteristics in the year of assignment: log employment rate of men aged 18-60, log employment rate of non-Western immigrant men aged 18-60, log percentage non-Western immigrant men aged 18-60, log employment rate of co-national men aged 18-60 and log percentage co-national men aged 18-60. These coefficient estimates are also reported in appendix Table A2 (see columns 2-6). Again, there is no systematic correlation between the observed family characteristics and any of these area characteristics. Remember that while age, number of children, and marital status was observed by the authorities before allocation, education was not.

A related question is whether some individuals were more likely to realize their preferred neighborhood choice than others. I investigate this question by analyzing whether the decision to move away from the neighborhood of assignment was affected by their educational attainment at the time of assignment, conditional on demographic individual characteristics as well as characteristics of the neighborhood of assignment and municipality of assignment. The results are reported in Table 7. There are no significant differences in the probability of moving neighborhood between educational groups. Inclusion of neighborhood of assignment characteristics increases the explanatory power from 7.5% (column 1) to 11.0% (column 7). In particular, the probability of neighborhood relocation decreases with assignment to a socially deprived neighborhood, the log of the employment rate of non-Western immigrant men aged 18-60 living in the neighborhood of assignment and the log of the employment rate of co-national men aged 18-60 living in the neighborhood of assignment. These results suggest that refugee men derive high utility from living in a socially deprived neighborhood (which is partly explained by their preference for living close to other non-Western immigrants and access to large and high-quality public housing apartments) and close to employed non-Western immigrant men and co-national men.

These results provide strong support for the refugee dispersal policy being quasi-random. Therefore, an indicator for assignment to a socially deprived neighborhood should be a valid instrument for current residence in a socially deprived neighborhood controlling for observed family characteristics, country of origin and year of immigration.

Another important issue is whether the indicator for assignment to a socially deprived neighborhood is a strong predictor for current residence in a socially deprived neighborhood up to six years after assignment. This depends on the extent to which refugees stayed in the neighborhood of assignment. As shown in appendix Table A3, six years after assignment 50% of individuals in the balanced sample of refugee men were still living in the municipality of assignment of which 28.8% were still living in the neighborhood of assignment. According to Table 7, assignment to a socially deprived neighborhood increased the probability of staying in the neighborhood of assignment by 15.5 percentage points. Moreover, for neighborhood movers, assignment to a socially deprived neighborhood significantly increased the probability of moving to another socially deprived neighborhood. Further investigation shows that this effect is entirely driven by individuals who moved to another neighborhood within the municipality of assignment. For those individuals, assignment to a socially deprived neighborhood increased the probability of moving to another socially deprived neighborhood by 9.8 percentage points, controlling for individual characteristics.[22] Therefore, I expect that the indicator for assignment to a socially deprived neighborhood is a strong predictor for current residence in a socially deprived neighborhood up to six years after assignment.

IV.C Instrumental variables model

The instrumental variables model is given by

(3)
$$y^*_{ijk(t+s)} = \alpha D_{ijk(t+s)} + X_{it}\beta + V_{j^*}\gamma + \delta_k + \delta_t + \delta_s + \delta_{j^*} + \mu_i + \varepsilon_{ijk(t+s)}$$

where the variables and indices are the same as in equation 2 if nothing else is stated below. The index s denotes years since assignment (s=2, ..., 6), δ_s are fixed effects for years since assignment and μ_i are individual-specific random effects which control for unobserved, time-invariant individual characteristics like innate abilities. The IV models are estimated using two different specifications. Specification 1 is the same as equation 3, except for exclusion of municipality of assignment fixed effects. That is, specification 1 uses both within and between municipality variation in neighborhood characteristics to identify the effect of living in a socially deprived neighborhood. By contrast, specification 2 is given in equation 3 and includes municipality of assignment fixed effects δ_{j^*}, i.e. relies only on within municipality variation in neighborhood characteristics. This means that specification 2 compares labor market outcomes of individuals assigned to different types of neighborhoods within the same municipality. In

---

[22] These results are available upon request.

other words, specification 2 controls for any unobserved time-invariant municipality characteristic which affects individual labor market outcomes. Therefore, specification 2 is a strong strategy for identification of neighborhood effects.

The main identification challenge is to take into account that $D_{ijk(t+s)}$ is an endogenous explanatory variable. Refugees could move away from the neighborhood of assignment any time after initial assignment as long as they were able to find alternative housing and the relocation decision is likely to be influenced by unobserved, time-varying individual characteristics like host-country and English language skills which also influence the individual's employment probability. Therefore, I instrument $D_{ijk(t+s)}$ by an indicator for individual i having been assigned to a socially deprived neighborhood in municipality j^* in year t denoted D_{ij^*kt}. The identifying assumption is that neighborhood assignment is random, conditional on family composition, source country and year of immigration. Under the assumption of homogenous treatment effects, the IV estimate of α is the average treatment effect of living in a socially deprived neighborhood for individuals in the balanced sample of refugee men.

Summary statistics of the dependent variable for the overall balanced sample of refugee men and by treatment status are shown in appendix Table A4. Six years after immigration 30.6% of refugee men have a job and the average real annual earnings of refugee men with wage income was DKK 62,318 (in 2000-prices).[23]

Panel A of Table 8 shows the coefficient estimates of living in a socially deprived neighborhood 2-6 years after immigration. Inclusion of individual-specific random effects in equation 3 decreases the magnitude of the estimates relative to the estimates of equation 2 reported in Table 4, but the coefficient estimates remains significant and negative. These estimates are those one would obtain using the observational data approach.

Panel B of Table 8 shows the estimated effects of assignment to a socially deprived neighborhood on the employment probability 2-6 years after immigration (in columns 1-2) and on log real annual earnings 2-6 years after immigration (in columns 5-6) for the two different specifications. These estimates show the effects of the policy of random

---

[23] For comparison, in 2000, 84% of men aged 20-59 in Denmark was employed (www.Statistikbanken.dk/RASA and BEF5) and their mean real annual earnings were DKK 238,294 (www.Statistikbanken.dk/ INDKP1).

assignment across socially deprived and non-deprived neighborhoods. Therefore, they can be interpreted as intent-to-treat estimates. There are no significant differences in the employment probability and real annual earnings of individuals in the treatment and control group 2-6 years after immigration. In other words, assignment to a socially deprived neighborhood did neither affect the employment probability nor real annual earnings of refugees 2-6 years after assignment.

Next, I estimate the average treatment effect (ATE) of living in a socially deprived neighborhood on individual labor market outcomes using two-stage least squares (2SLS). I instrument the indicator for living in a socially deprived neighborhood 2-6 years after immigration by an indicator for assignment to a socially deprived neighborhood. The first stage regression estimates of the instrument on the endogenous explanatory variable are reported in Panel C in Table 8. For the overall sample, ceteris paribus, assignment to a socially deprived neighborhood significantly increases the probability of living in a socially deprived neighborhood 2-6 years after immigration by 24.2% (t-statistic of 10), i.e. the instrument is a strong predictor of the endogenous explanatory variable. The 2SLS estimates of living in a socially deprived neighborhood 2-6 years after immigration on individual labor market outcomes are also reported in Panel C of Table 8; the 2SLS estimates are positive, but insignificant.

I interpret the insignificant 2SLS estimates of living in a socially deprived neighborhood as evidence that the negative and significant statistical associations between living in a socially deprived neighborhood and individual labor market outcomes (reported in Panel A of Table 8 and in Table 4) are entirely due to negative self-selection of individuals (e.g. individuals with poor host-country and English language skills) into socially deprived neighborhoods. Controlling for individual self-selection into neighborhoods, living in a socially deprived neighborhood does not affect individual labor market outcomes.

An obvious criticism of my analysis is that the 60% employment rate threshold used to categorize neighborhoods as socially deprived and non-deprived is somewhat arbitrary. Therefore, I estimate an alternative model, in which the bivariate explanatory variable "living in a socially deprived neighborhood", $D_{ijk(t+s)}$, in equation 3 is replaced by the continuous variable "the log of the employment rate of men aged 18-60 living in the neighborhood of residence". I estimate the ATE of the log of the employment rate of men aged 18-60 living in the neighborhood of residence" by 2SLS using the log employment rate of men aged 18-60 living the neighborhood of assignment as instrument. As shown in Panel C of Table 9, the instrument is a strong predictor: Using the specification with municipality of assignment fixed effects, a log increase in the employment rate of men aged 18-60 living in the neighborhood of assignment increases the log of the employment rate of men aged 18-60 in the neighborhood of residence 2-6 years after assignment by 0.309 (t-statistic of 8.2) in the employment model 2 and by 0.236 (t-statistic of 8.6) in the earnings model. However, as shown in Panel B of Table 9, the intent-to-treat estimates are close to zero and insignificant. Recall that the 2SLS estimate is defined as the intent-to-treat estimate (reported in Panel B) divided by the first-stage regression estimate (reported in Panel C). Therefore, the insignificant intent-to-treat estimates translates into insignificant 2SLS estimates of the log employment rate of men aged 18-60 living in the neighborhood of residence on the employment probability (columns 1-2) and log of real annual earnings (columns 5-6) reported in Panel C of Table 9. In other words, the employment rate of men living in neighborhood of residence does neither affect the employment probability of refugee men, nor their real annual earnings 2-6 years after immigration. The results from separate estimation of low-skilled and highly skilled men are reported in columns 3-4 and 7-8 of Table 9. As for the full sample, the 2SLS estimates are insignificant for both skill groups.

Since the 2SLS estimates reported in Panel C of Table 9 are insignificant, the positive and significant correlations between the log employment rate of men aged 18-60 living in the neighborhood of residence and individual labor market outcomes 2-6 years after immigration (reported in the Panel A of Table 9) must be due to positive self-selection of individuals into neighborhoods with a relatively high employment rate of men aged 18-60.

In the next subsection, I estimate alternative models of neighborhood effects.

IV.D Ethnic stratification of networks

Recall from Section II.A that 26.3% of immigrants in the Welfare Research Survey had found their latest (wage earner) job through their social network. Panel C of Table 2 shows that 74.7% (87.2% of low-skilled) of immigrant survey respondents who found their latest job through their social network found it through other immigrants. This descriptive evidence suggests that immigrants interact primarily with neighbors of immigrant origin. If so, the employment rate of non-Western immigrant men is a better measure of the employment rate of contacts of refugee men.

Therefore, I estimate the model in equation 3, except that $D_{ijk(t+s)}$ is replaced by the log employment rate of non-Western immigrant men aged 18-60 living in the neighborhood of residence 2-6 years after immigration. I instrument the log employment rate of non-Western immigrant men aged 18-60 living in the neighborhood of residence 2-6 years after immigration by the log employment rate of non-Western immigration men aged 18-60 living in the neighborhood of assignment and an indicator for no other non-Western immigrant men aged 18-60 living in the neighborhood of assignment in the year of assignment. The 2SLS results are reported in Panel B of Table 10. Both instruments are strong predictors of the log employment rate of men aged 18-60 living in the neighborhood of residence. Using specification 2, a log increase in the employment rate of non-Western immigrants living in the neighborhood of assignment increases the log employment rate of non-Western immigrants living in the current neighborhood of residence by 0.031 (t-statistic of 6.0) in the employment model and by 0.028 (t-statistic of 5.1) in the earnings model. According to the 2SLS estimates, the log employment rate of non-Western immigrant men aged 18-60 living in the neighborhood of residence has a positive and significant effect on the individual's employment probability as well as on real annual earnings. Separate results for low- and highly skilled men are reported in columns 3-4 (employment model) and columns 8-9 (earnings model) of Table 10. The 2SLS estimates are positive for both skill groups and significant for highly skilled. Around the mean of 36.8%, a percentage point increase in the employment rate of non-Western immigrant men aged 18-60 living in the neighborhood of residence corresponds to 0.03 of a log increase. This implies that, on average, a percentage point increase in the employment rate of non-Western immigrant men aged 18-60 living in the neighborhood of residence (around the mean) increases the individual's employment probability by (0.03*0.065=) 0.2 percentage points and log real annual earnings by (0.03*0.808=) 0.02, corresponding to a 2% increase in real annual earnings 2-6 years after immigration.

As seen from the 2SLS estimates reported in columns 6 and 12 of Panel B in Table 10, these results are robust to inclusion of the log of the percentage non-Western immigrant men aged 18-60 living in the neighborhood of residence 2-6 years after immigration (instrumented by the log of the percentage non-Western immigrant men aged 18-60 living in the neighborhood of assignment). Moreover, according to the 2SLS estimate reported in column 6, the log percentage non-Western immigrant men aged 18-60 living in the neighborhood of residence decreases the individual's employment probability 2-6 years after immigration. However, the effect turns insignificant after inclusion of the interaction between the log employment rate of non-Western immigrant men and the log percentage non-Western immigrant men aged 18-60 living in the neighborhood of residence 2-6 years after immigration (see column 7 in Table 10).[24]

The results in Table 10 provide strong evidence of neighborhood effects, in particular that non-Western immigrant men in part find jobs through employed contacts of non-Western immigrant origin living in the neighborhood of residence. But are all employed contacts of non-Western immigrant origin in the neighborhood equally useful for finding a (well-paid) job? Or are employed contacts from the individual's own source country (henceforth referred to as co-nationals) particularly valuable? I investigate this question by estimating the 2SLS estimate of the log of the employment rate of co-national men aged 18-60 living in the neighborhood of residence using the same model as equation 3, except that $D_{ijk(t+s)}$ is replaced by the log employment rate of co-national men aged 18-60 living in the neighborhood of residence 2-6 years after immigration. As instruments I use the log of the employment rate of co-national men aged 18-60 in the neighborhood of assignment and an indicator for no other co-national men aged 18-60 living in the neighborhood assignment in the year of assignment as instruments. The 2SLS results for the overall sample using two different specifications (without and with municipality of assignment fixed effects) are reported in Panel B of Table 11, columns 1-2 (employment model) and 8-9 (earnings model). Both instruments have strong predictive power in the first stage of the employment model, whereas in the earnings model only the second

---

[24] As instrument for the interaction variable, I use the interaction between the log employment rate of non-Western immigrant men and the log percentage non-Western immigrant men aged 18-60 living in the neighborhood of assignment. The instrument is a strong predictor in both models (employment and earnings models).

instrument has strong predictive power. According to the 2SLS estimates, the log employment rate of co-national men aged 18-60 living in the neighborhood of residence has a positive, but insignificant effect on the individual's employment probability, and a positive and significant effect on individual real annual earnings. One percentage point increase in the employment rate of co-national men aged 18-60 living in the neighborhood of residence 2-6 years after immigration (around the sample mean of 23.2%) corresponds to a log increase of 0.04 and therefore increases log real annual earnings by (0.04*0.407=) 0.02, or real annual earnings by 2%. The effect is of the same magnitude for low- and highly skilled (see columns 10-11 in Table 11).

I also investigate whether the size of the co-ethnic network in the neighborhood affects individual labor market outcomes. I do so by estimating the effect of the log of the percentage co-national men aged 18-60 living in the neighborhood of residence using 2SLS. The set of controls is the same as in equation 3. As instruments I use the log of the percentage co-national men aged 18-60 and an indicator for no other co-national men living in the neighborhood of assignment. The results are presented in columns 5 and 10 of Table 11. The first instrument is a strong predictor; the t-statistic is 3.5 in the employment model and 3.2 in the earnings model. According to the 2SLS estimates in Panel B of Table 11, columns 5 and 10, the log percentage co-national men aged 18-60 living in the neighborhood of residence has a positive, but insignificant effect on the individual's employment probability, and a positive and significant effect (at a 10% significance level) on log real annual earnings. The latter result is very interesting. It suggests that the finding of Edin et al. (2003) and Damm (2009) of a positive effect of ethnic enclave size on individual real annual earnings can be interpreted as a neighborhood effect.

However, the size and the quality of the local ethnic enclave are positively correlated because larger ethnic enclaves are more established. Therefore, the positive and significant effect of log percentage co-nationals aged 18-60 living in the neighborhood of residence on the individual's real annual earnings 2-6 years after immigration may ve upward biased due to omission of ethnic enclave quality. To test this hypothesis, I add the log employment rate of co-national men aged 18-60 living in the neighborhood of residence 2-6 years after immigration as an additional explanatory variable to the model with the log of percent co-national men aged 18-60 living in the neighborhood of residence 2-6 years after immigration. As instruments I use the log employment rate of co-national men aged 18-60 living, the log percentage co-national men aged 18-60 and an indicator for no other co-national men aged 18-60 living in the neighborhood of assignment in the year of assignment. The results are presented in columns 6 and 13 of Table 11.[25] According to the 2SLS estimates reported in Panel B, the 2SLS estimate of the log percentage co-national men aged 18-60 living in the neighborhood of residence 2-6 years after immigration approaches zero in the employment model and turns negative, but insignificant in the earnings model in response to inclusion of the log employment rate of co-national men aged 18-60 living in the neighborhood of residence. By contrast, the 2SLS estimate of the log employment rate of co-national men aged 18-60 living in the neighborhood of residence on real annual earnings 2-6 years after immigration remains positive and significant and increases slightly in magnitude relative to the model without the log percentage co-national men aged 18-60 living in the neighborhood of residence reported in columns 8 and 9 of Table 11. These findings provide quasi-experimental evidence that it is the quality - not the size - of the co-ethnic network living in the neighborhood that matters for the individual's real annual earnings.

Finally, I test whether it is the quality of non-Western immigrant contacts or the quality of the co-ethnic network that matters for the individual's labor market outcomes. I do so by estimating the effect of the log employment rate of non-Western immigrant men aged 18-60 and the log employment rate of co-national men aged 18-60 who live in the municipality of residence on individual labor market outcomes 2-6 years after immigration by 2SLS.[26] The 2SLS estimates are reported in Panel B of Table 11 (columns 7 and 14). Recall from Table 10, column 2, that the employment effect of the log employment rate of non-Western immigrants living in the neighborhood of residence is positive and significant. The 2SLS estimates reported in Table 11, column 7, show that the positive employment effect of the log employment rate of non-Western immigrant

---

[25] With t-statistics between 3 and 4, all instrumental variables are strong predictors in the employment model, and the two last-mentioned instrumental variables are strong predictors in the earnings model.

[26] As instrument I use the log employment rate of non-Western immigrant men aged 18-60 and the log employment rate of co-national men aged 18-60 who live in the municipality of assignment in the year of assignment as well as two indicators for no other non-Western immigrant men aged 18-60 and no other co-national men aged 18-60 living in the municipality of assignment in the year of assignment. The instrument has strong predictive power.

men living in the neighborhood of residence decreases in response to inclusion of the log employment rate of co-national men living in the neighborhood of residence as an additional explanatory variable. Similarly, the positive 2SLS estimate of the log employment rate of co-national men living in the neighborhood of residence on the individual's employment probability (reported in column 2, Table 11) decreases in response to inclusion of the log employment rate of non-Western immigrant men living in the neighborhood of residence as an additional explanatory variable. These findings suggest that the individual's employment probability is positively affected by a high employment rate of both non-Western immigrant men and co-national men aged 18-60 living in the neighborhood of residence. The 2SLS estimates reported in Table 11, column 14, show that the finding of a positive and significant earnings effect of log of the employment rate of co-national men aged 18-60 living the neighborhood of residence reported in Table 11, columns 8 and 9, is robust to inclusion of the log employment rate of non-Western immigrant men living in the neighborhood of residence as an additional explanatory variable; the magnitude of the 2SLS estimate is virtually unchanged. By contrast, the estimate of the earnings effect of log employment rate of non-Western immigrant men aged 18-60 living in the neighborhood reported in Table 10 approaches zero and becomes insignificant in response to inclusion of the log employment rate of co-national men aged 18-60 living in the neighborhood. I interpret the 2SLS estimates reported in Table 11, column 14, as evidence that immigrant real annual earnings are positively affected by the employment rate of co-national men aged 18-60 living in the neighborhood of residence and not affected by the employment rate of non-Western immigrant men from other source countries living in the neighborhood of residence.

My findings of i) a positive employment effect of a log increase in the employment rate of non-Western immigrant men aged 18-60 living in the neighborhood (reported in Table 10) and ii) a positive earnings effect of a log increase in the employment rate of co-national men aged 18-60 living in the neighborhood of residence (reported in Table 11) are robust to exclusion of refugees who were assigned to Copenhagen City. This is seen by comparison with the 2SLS estimates for this subsample reported in Table 12.

Moreover, further investigation shows that the positive and significant 2SLS estimates of the log employment rate of the non-Western immigrant network and of the co-ethnic network in the neighborhood reported in Tables 9 and 10, respectively, are homogenous both across years since assignment and country of origin.[27]

Summing up, the 2SLS estimates of various neighborhood characteristics presented in this section of the paper is strong evidence that labor market outcomes of refugee men of non-Western origin 2-6 years after immigration i) are not influenced by residence in a socially deprived neighborhood, ii) are not influenced by the log of the employment rate of men aged 18-60 living in the neighborhood of residence, iii) are positively affected by the log of the employment rate of non-Western immigrant men aged 18-60 living in the neighborhood of residence (also after inclusion of the log percentage non-Western immigrant men aged 18-60 living in the neighborhood of residence). I interpret these results as evidence that residence-based networks are ethnically stratified as suggested by e.g. Hellerstein, McInerney and Neumark (2011).

Furthermore, individual log real annual earnings are positively affected by i) the log of the employment rate of co-national men aged 18-60 living in the neighborhood of residence (also after inclusion of the log percentage co-national men aged 18-60 in percent of men aged 18-60 living in the neighborhood of residence), and ii) the log percentage co-national men aged 18-60 in percent of men aged 18-60 living in the neighborhood of residence, but the latter 2SLS estimate turns insignificant if the log employment rate of co-national men aged 18-60 living in the neighborhood of residence is included in the model. Overall, I interpret my quasi-experimental findings as evidence that non-Western immigrants find jobs in part through their employed contacts of non-Western immigrant and co-ethnic origin living in their neighborhood and that the individual's employment probability and annual earnings increase with the quality of contacts.

V. Conclusion

It is a stylized fact that a substantial share of workers finds jobs through personal contacts. However, little is known about which types of contacts are useful in job search. My results shed substantial light on this issue. I use two different strategies to identify the effects of the quality and quantity of strong and weak ties taking into account individual

---

[27] The results are available from the author upon request.

self-selection into social networks, i.e. that people are more likely to become friends or acquainted with people with similar demographic characteristics and socio-economic background. Using self-reported information about characteristics of personal contacts, I find for unemployed survey respondents that having acquaintances of which the majority are employed significantly increases the individual's job-finding rate, whereas the effect of the number of acquaintances is insignificant.

My quasi-experimental neighborhood effects for refugee men of non-Western origin provide further evidence of the positive influence of employed acquaintances. A percentage point increase (around the mean) in the employment rate of non-Western immigrant men aged 18-60 living in the neighborhood of residence increases the employment probability of refugee men of non-Western origin by 0.2 percentage points, or 0.7%. Similarly, a percentage point increase (around the mean) in the employment rate of co-national men aged 18-60 living in the neighborhood of residence increases real annual earnings of refugee men by 2%. The results are robust to inclusion of the percentage non-Western immigrant men and percentage co-national men living in the neighborhood of residence. A potential explanation for these asymmetric findings is that while employed contacts of non-Western immigrant origin are useful for finding a job in the host-country, employed co-national contacts are useful for finding a job which matches the individual's skills, because only co-nationals know the value of the individual's education obtained in the country of origin. That is, co-national contacts disseminate information which increases the job-worker match quality and thereby the hourly wage rate (for theoretical and empirical evidence on this mechanism, see Damm, 2009, and Dustmann, Glitz and Schönberg, 2011).

Overall, my findings provide strong evidence that the quality of acquaintances (including neighbors of similar gender and ethnic origin) influences individual labor market outcomes: the higher the employment rate of acquaintances, the easier it is to find a job and the better paid it is. These findings suggest that unemployed individuals with more employed contacts receive more informal information about job vacancies. By contrast, overall my findings lend little support to the view that the number of acquaintances should have an effect.

The results have important policy implications for labor market integration of immigrants. Policy makers in countries in which the authorities disperse newly recognized refugees across regions can use this result for optimal design. Previous research on spatial dispersal of refugees emphasizes the importance of refugee settlement in regions with a low unemployment rate (Åslund and Rooth, 2007). In view of the results of this paper, policy makers should also help refugees find housing in neighborhoods with established immigrant networks because these promote labor market outcomes of new immigrants. More generally, the results suggest that successful local employment policies targeted at a subgroup of immigrants entail positive externalities for their immigrant acquaintances.

References

Addison, John T. and Pedro Portugal. 2002. Job Search Methods and Outcomes. *Oxford Economic Papers,* vol. 54: 505-533.

Andersen, Hans Skifter. 2005. Den sociale og etniske udvikling i almene boligafdelinger (SBI 2005:10). København: Statens Byggeforskningsinstitut.

Andersson, Fredrik, Simon Burgess and Julia Lane. 2009. Do as the Neighbors Do: The Impact of Social Networks on Immigrant Employment. IZA DP no. 4423.

Bayer, Patrick, Stephen L. Ross and Giorgio Topa. 2008. Place of Work and Place of Residence: Informal Hiring Networks and Labor Market Outcomes. *Journal of Political Economy,* vol. 116(6): 1150-1196.

Bentolila, Samuel, Claudio Michelacci and Javier Suárez. 2010. Social Contacts and Occupational Choice. *Economica,* vol. 77: 20-45.

Blau, David M. and Philip K. Robins. 1990. Job Search Outcomes for the Employed and Unemployed. *Journal of Political Economy,* vol. 98(3): 637-655.

Calvó-Armengol, Antoni and Matthew O. Jackson. 2004. The Effects of Social Networks on Employment and Inequality. *American Economic Review*, vol. 94(3) (Jun.): 426-454.

Coleman, David and Eskil Wadensjö. 1999. *Indvandringen til Danmark. Internationale og nationale perspektiver.* Spektrum.

Damm, Anna P. 2009. Ethnic Enclaves and Immigrant Labor Market Outcomes: Quasi-Experimental Evidence. *Journal of Labor Economics*, vol. 27(2): 281-314.

Damm, Anna P. and Marie L. Schultz-Nielsen. 2008. Danish Neighborhoods: Construction and Relevance for Measurement of Residential Segregation. *Nationaløkonomisk Tidsskrift (Danish Economic Journal),* vol. 146: 241-262.

Damm, Anna P., Marie L. Schultz-Nielsen and Torben Tranæs. 2006. *En befolkning deler sig op?* Denmark: Gyldendal.

Danish Refugee Council, *Annual Report*, 1986–1996.

Danish Refugee Council, *Administrativ Statistik* [Administrative statistics], 1992–1997.

Danish Refugee Council, Central Integration Unit (CIU), *Dansk Flygtningehjælps integrationsarbejde* [Danish Refugee Council Integration Policy], 1996.

Deding, Mette, Torben Fridberg and Vibeke Jakobsen. 2008. Non-response in a survey among immigrants in Denmark. *Survey Research Methods*, vol. 2(3): 107-121.

Dustmann, Christian, Albrecht Glitz and Uta Schönberg. 2011. Referral-based Job Search Networks. Norface Migration Discussion Paper No. 2011-12.

Edin, Per-Anders, Peter Fredriksson and Oluf Åslund. 2003. Ethnic Enclaves and the Economic Success of Immigrants - Evidence from a Natural Experiment. *Quarterly Journal of Economics,* vol. 118: 329-357.

Granovetter, Mark. 1973. The Strength of Weak Ties, *American Journal of Sociology,* vol. 78(6) (May):1360-80.

Granovetter, Mark. 1974, 1995. *Getting a Job: A Study of Contacts and Careers*, Chicago: University of Chicago Press.

Gregg, Paul and Jonathan Wadsworth. 1996. How Effective are State Employment Agencies? Jobcentre Use and Job Matching in Britain. *Oxford Bulletin of Economics and Statistics*, vol. 58(3): 443-467.

Hellerstein, Judith K., Melissa McInerney and David Neumark. Neighbors and Co-workers: The Importance of Residential Labor Market Networks. *Journal of Labor Economics*, vol. 29(4): 659-695.

Holzer, Harry J. 1988. Search Methods Use by Unemployed Youth. *Journal of Labor Economics*, vol. 6(1): 1-20.

Ioannides, Yannis M. and Linda Datcher Loury. 2004. Job Information Networks, Neighborhood Effects, and Inequality. *Journal of Economic Literature*, vol. 42(4) (Dec.): 1056-1093.

Jacob, Brian A. 2004. Public Housing, Housing Vouchers, and Student Achievement: Evidence from Public Housing Demolitions in Chicago. *American Economic Review*, vol. 94(1) (Mar.): 233-258.

Mogensen, Gunnar V. and Poul Chr. Matthiessen. 2000. *Integration i Danmark omkring årtusindskiftet.* Aarhus Universitetsforlag.

Mogensen, Gunnar V. and Poul Chr. Matthiessen. 2002. *Indvandrerne og arbejdsmarkedet. Mødet med det danske velfærdssamfund.* Spektrum.

Montgomery, James D. 1991. Social Networks and Labor-Market Outcomes: Toward an Economic Analysis. *American Economic Review*, vol. 81(5) (Dec.): 1408-1418.

Montgomery, James D. 1994. Weak Ties, Employment, and Inequality: An Equilibrium Analysis. *American Journal of Sociology*, vol. 99(5) (Mar.): 1212-1236.

Munshi, Kaivan. 2003. Networks in the Modern Economy: Mexican Migrants in the US Labor Market". *Quarterly Journal of Economics*, vol. 118(2): 549-599.

Oreopoulos, Philip. 2003. The Long-Run Consequences of Living in a Poor Neighborhood. *Quarterly Journal of Economics*, vol. 118(4) (Nov.): 1533-1575.

Pellizari, Michele. 2010. Do Friends and Relatives really Help in Getting a Good Job? *Industrial and Labor Relations Review*, vol. 63(3): 494-510.

Rees. Albert. 1966. Labor Economics: Effects of More Knowledge. Information Networks in Labor Market. *American Economic Review*, (Papers and Proceedings), vol. 56 (½) (Mar. 1.): 559-566.

Statistics Denmark. 1992, 1997, 2000. *Statistisk Årbog* 1992, 1997, 2000 (Statistical Yearbook 1992, 1997, 2000). Copenhagen: Statistics Denmark.

Topa, Giorgio. 2001. Social Interactions, Local Spillovers and Unemployment. *Review of Economic Studies*, vol. 68(2) (Apr.): 261-295.

Wahba, Jackline and Yves Zenou. 2005. Density, Social Networks and Job Search Methods: Theory and Application to Egypt. *Journal of Development Economics*, vol. 78: 443-473.

Weinberg, Bruce A., Patricia B. Reagan and Jeffrey J. Yankow. 2004. Do Neighborhoods Affect Hours Worked? Evidence from Longitudinal Data. *Journal of Labor Economics*, vol. 22(4): 891-924.

www.Statistikbanken.dk/RASA, BEF5 and INDKP1.

Åslund, Oluf and Dan-Oluf Rooth. 2007. Do When and Where Matter? Initial Labour Market Conditions and Immigrant Earnings. *The Economic Journal*, vol. 117 (Mar.): 422-448.

Table 1.A: Summary statistics of sample of survey respondents.

	All		Unemployed	
	Danes	Immigrants	Danes	Immigrants
	1	2	3	4
Woman	0.529	0.448	0.739	0.62
	(0.500)	(0.498)	(0.442)	(0.490)
Age	32.6	34.0	32.2	34.6
	(7.7)	(7.5)	(7.3)	(6.9)
Married	0.42	0.685	0.435	0.738
	(0.494)	(0.465)	(0.499)	(0.441)
Child aged 0-2	0.181	0.199	0.319	0.278
	(0.385)	(0.399)	(0.469)	(0.449)
Child aged 3-17	0.487	0.611	0.493	0.711
	(0.5)	(0.488)	(0.504)	(0.454)
Educational attainment:				
0-9 years of education	0.009	0.231	0	0.399
	(0.095)	(0.422)		(0.491)
10-12 years of education	0.651	0.493	0.841	0.407
	(0.477)	(0.500)	(0.369)	(0.492)
More than 12 years of education	0.34	0.275	0.159	0.194
	(0.474)	(0.447)	(0.369)	(0.396)
Unknown educational attainment	0	0.001	0	0
		(0.036)		
Immigration year	-	1989.4	-	1990.9
		(8.1)		(8.2)
Country of origin:				
Denmark	1	0	1	0
Iran	0	0.389	0	0.316
		(0.488)		(0.466)
Turkey	0	0.35	0	0.426
		(0.477)		(0.495)
Pakistan	0	0.262	0	0.259
		(0.440)		(0.439)
Labor market outcomes:				
Employed in Nov. 2006/2007	0.923	0.764	0.652	491
	(0.266)	(0.425)	(0.480)	(0.501)
Work experience since 1980 (full-time years)	6.83	3.13	4.38	2.14
	(8.45)	(4.25)	(6.21)	(3.30)
Municipality of residence characteristics:				
Log(inhabitants)	10.65	11.41	10.40	11.52
	(1.38)	(1.24)	(1.42)	(1.30)
Log(mean gross income)	12.31	12.30	12.29	12.28
	(0.10)	(0.10)	(0.08)	(0.08)
Unemployment rate	4.60	4.90	4.99	5.10
	(1.45)	(1.16)	(1.81)	(1.11)
N	874	1575	69	263

Table 1.B: Summary statistics of sample of survey respondents.

	All		Unemployed	
	Danes	Immigrants	Danes	Immigrants
	1	2	3	4
Employed in the week before the interview	0.763 (0.425)	0.596 (0.491)	0	0
Proficient in Danish	-	0.634 (0.482)	-	0.456 (0.500)
Proficient in English	0.882 (0.323)	0.56 (0.497)	0.826 (0.382)	0.35 (0.478)
Reason for immigration:				
Family-reunification with spouse	-	0.345 (0.476)	-	0.217 (0.413)
Family-reunification with parents	-	0.283 (0.451)	-	0.483 (0.501)
Refugee	-	0.291 (0.454)	-	0.232 (0.423)
Work or education in Denmark (DK)	-	0.04 (0.196)	-	0.03 (0.172)
Other	-	0.034 (0.182)	-	0.03 (0.172)
Network size:				
Number of acquaintances in DK	34.82 (26.35)	29.28 (25.68)	26.45 (23.04)	25.43 (24.99)
Number of acquaintances in DK above average	0.443 (0.497)	0.387 (0.487)	0.319 (0.469)	0.33 (0.47)
Majority of immigrant acquaintances in Denmark	-	0.268 (0.443)	-	0.384 (0.487)
High employment rate of:				
Family members in DK	0.954 (0.209)	0.58 (0.494)	0.928 (0.261)	0.517 (0.501)
Close friends in DK	0.935 (0.247)	0.795 (0.404)	0.884 (0.323)	0.726 (0.447)
Acquaintances in DK	0.891 (0.311)	0.78 (0.414)	0.812 (0.394)	0.722 (0.449)
High level of education of:				
Family members in DK	0.891 (0.311)	0.391 (0.488)	0.841 (0.369)	0.274 (0.447)
Close friends in DK	0.852 (0.355)	0.563 (0.496)	0.797 (0.405)	0.453 (0.498)
Acquaintances in DK	0.736 (0.441)	0.48 (0.500)	0.696 (0.464)	0.361 (0.481)
N	874	1575	69	263

Table 1.B: Summary statistics of sample of survey respondents (continued).

	All		Unemployed	
	Danes	Immigrants	Danes	Immigrants
	1	2	3	4
Work attitude: Work primarily to earn a living	0.421	0.677	0.478	0.73
	(0.494)	(0.468)	(0.503)	(0.445)
Unemployed individuals should be willing to move to get a permanent job:				
View of respondent:	0.338	0.489	0.188	0.418
	(0.494)	(0.500)	(0.394)	(0.494)
View of family in DK	0.336	0.225	0.188	0.186
	(0.473)	(0.418)	(0.394)	(0.39)
View of close friends in DK	0.305	0.298	0.159	0.243
	(0.461)	(0.457)	(0.369)	(0.430)
Unemployed individuals ought to be willing to work at a salary below the incomes as unemployed:				
View of respondent	0.315	0.354	0.232	0.285
	(0.465)	(0.478)	(0.425)	(0.452)
View of family in DK	0.292	0.17	0.174	0.107
	(0.455)	(0.376)	(0.382)	(0.309)
View of close friends in DK	0.227	0.198	0.145	0.148
	(0.419)	(0.399)	(0.355)	(0.356)
It is humiliating to receive social assistance:				
View of respondent	0.243	0.482	0.304	0.449
	(0.429)	(0.500)	(0.464)	(0.498)
View of family in DK	0.263	0.282	0.275	0.213
	(0.441)	(0.450)	(0.500)	(0.410)
View of close friends in DK	0.22	0.333	0.232	0.319
	(0.414)	(0.472)	(0.425)	(0.467)
N	874	1575	69	263

Note: Missing values of educational attainment information in the administrative registers have been replaced by educational attainment information from the Welfare Research Survey conducted by SFI Survey in 2006 in Denmark.

Source: Panel A: Administrative register data from Statistics Denmark, Panel B: Welfare Research Survey conducted by SFI Survey in Denmark in 2006.

Table 2: Summary statistics of means of finding the latest job. Survey respondents who were in the labor force one week before the interview and who work/have worked as an employee.

	Danes	Immigrants		
	All	All	Low-skilled	Highly skilled
	1	2	3	4
Panel A: Means of finding the latest job (%)				
Direct search channel	70.5	66.7	60.3	68.7
Network	16.6	26.3	36.0	23.3
Other	12.9	7	3.8	8.0
Sum	100.0	100.0	100.1	100.0
N	668	987	239	747
Panel B: Direct search channel used to find the latest job (%)				
Employment agency	13.8	28.7	44.4	24.4
Direct application to employer	44.2	44.2	38.2	45.8
Temp agency	1.5	2	1.4	2.1
Spare time job	0.2	0.8	0.7	0.8
Reply to job advertisement in the media	40.3	24.2	15.3	26.7
Unknown	0	0.1	0	0.2
Sum	100.0	100.0	100.0	100.0
N	471	658	144	513
Panel C: Network channel used to find the latest job (%)				
Danish relatives	19.1	1.5	0	2.3
Danish close friends	47.3	14.6	5.8	18.9
Danish acquaintances	33.6	8.1	5.8	9.2
Relatives of immigrant origin		35.8	41.9	32.8
Close friends of immigrant origin		31.2	36.0	28.7
Acquaintances of immigrant origin		7.7	9.3	6.9
Unknown		1.1	1.2	1.2
Sum	100.0	100.0	100.0	100.0
N	110	260	86	174

Note: Only four Danish respondents are low-skilled.
Source: Welfare Research Survey conducted by SFI Survey in Denmark in 2006.

Table 3: Coefficient estimates from linear regression of being employed in Nov. 2006 or Nov. 2007 on individual and area characteristics in 2006. Unemployed survey respondents.

	Danes				Immigrants				
	1	2	3	4	5	6	7	8	9
Danish language proficiency	-	-	-	-	0.165*	0.191**	0.196**	0.181**	0.189**
					(0.071)	(0.067)	(0.067)	(0.065)	(0.060)
English language proficiency	0.01	-0.048	-0.054	-0.197	0.288**	0.285**	0.282**	0.274**	0.244**
	(0.156)	(0.172)	(0.183)	(0.210)	(0.089)	(0.094)	(0.094)	(0.093)	(0.087)
Social network characteristics:									
Number of acquaintances	-	0.026	-0.005	0.055	-	0.005	-0.079	0.045	0.049
		(0.108)	(0.134)	(0.116)		(0.041)	(0.079)	(0.053)	(0.055)
No. acquaintances*high employment rate of acq.	-	-	0.035	-	-	-	0.105	-	-
			(0.173)				(0.083)		
No. acquaintances *majority of immigrant acq.	-	-	-	-	-	-	-	-0.085	-0.08
								(0.051)	(0.058)
Majority of immigrant acquaintances	-	-	-	-	-	-	-	-0.115†	-0.138**
								(0.068)	(0.068)
High employment rate of:									
Family in DK	-	-0.276	-0.269	-0.515	-	-0.118	-0.116	-0.116	-0.144†
		(0.343)	(0.350)	(0.296)		(0.071)	(0.071)	(0.072)	(0.081)
Close friends in DK	-	0.006	0.006	0.199	-	-0.041	-0.043	-0.042	-0.025
		(0.199)	(0.202)	(0.239)		(0.065)	(0.066)	(0.067)	(0.065)
Acquaintances in DK	-	0.410*	0.409*	0.488*	-	0.135†	0.176*	0.130*	0.119†
		(0.185)	(0.186)	(0.219)		(0.069)	(0.072)	(0.065)	(0.064)
High skill level of:									
Family in DK	-	0.277	0.276	0.341	-	0.039	0.033	0.032	0.016
		(0.167)	(0.170)	(0.219)		(0.077)	(0.080)	(0.079)	(0.080)
Close friends in DK	-	-0.266	-0.263	-0.381	-	0.004	0.013	-0.007	-0.021
		(0.194)	(0.200)	(0.192)		(0.077)	(0.080)	(0.077)	(0.071)
Acquaintances in DK	-	-0.031	-0.027	0.011	-	-0.024	-0.025	-0.019	-0.008
		(0.150)	(0.156)	(0.168)		(0.076)	(0.075)	(0.077)	(0.075)
Work attitude: Primarily work to earn a living	-	-	-	0.029	-	-	-	-	-0.135
				(0.159)					(0.089)
"Unemployed individuals should be willing to move to get a permanent job":									
View of respondent	-	-	-	-0.498**	-	-	-	-	-0.023
				(0.176)					(0.077)
View of family in DK	-	-	-	0.295	-	-	-	-	0.005
				(0.238)					(0.081)
"Unemployed individuals ought to be willing to work at a salary below the income as unemployed":									
View of respondent	-	-	-	0.252	-	-	-	-	0.022
				(0.195)					(0.094)
View of family in DK	-	-	-	-0.234	-	-	-	-	-0.053
				(0.265)					(0.117)
"It is humiliating to receive social assistance":									
View of respondent	-	-	-	-0.002	-	-	-	-	-0.124
				(0.223)					(0.088)
View of family in DK	-	-	-	-0.274	-	-	-	-	0.151
				(0.262)					(0.100)
R^2	0.213	0.300	0.300	0.400	0.290	0.324	0.327	0.336	0.358
N			69				263		

Note: **: P<0.01, *: P<0.05, †: P<0.1. Standard errors (reported in parentheses) are clustered by municipality of residence. Additional controls: indicators for gender, marital status, having a child aged 0-2, having a child aged 3-17, educational attainment (0-9 years or missing, 10-12 years or more than 12 years), work experience, work experience squared, interactions between female and married, female and a child aged 0-2 and female and a child aged 3-17, and socioeconomic characteristics of the municipality of residence (log(inhabitants), unemployment rate, log(average gross income)). Additional controls for immigrants: Indicators for year of immigration, country of origin and self-reported reason for immigration (family re-unification with spouse, family re-unification with parents, refugee, work or education in Denmark or other reason). Share of individuals who are employed in Nov. 2006 or 2007: Danes: 0.65 (0.48), immigrants: 0.49 (0.50).

Source: Welfare Research Survey conducted by SFI Survey in Denmark in 2006 linked with administrative registers from Statistics Denmark.

Table 4: Coefficient estimates (standard errors) from linear regression of individual labor market outcomes on an indicator for living in a socially deprived neighborhood six years after immigration. Balanced panel of male refugees.

	Dependent variable:											
	Employed in Nov.						Ln(real annual earnings)					
	All		Low-skilled		Highly skilled		All		Low-skilled		Highly skilled	
	1	2	3	4	5	6	7	8	9	10	11	12
Neighborhood of residence:												
Socially deprived	-0.045**	-0.045**	-0.022*	-0.023†	-0.063**	-0.063**	-0.101*	-0.095**	-0.054	-0.015	-0.142*	-0.140*
	(0.007)	(0.006)	(0.011)	(0.012)	(0.014)	(0.013)	(0.044)	(0.046)	(0.056)	(0.058)	(0.058)	(0.059)
Controls for area of assignment:												
Socio-economic and demographic municipality characteristics	Yes	Yes	Yes	Yes	Yes	Yes	Yes	Yes	Yes	Yes	Yes	Yes
Municipality of assignment FE	No	Yes	No	Yes	No	Yes	No	Yes	No	Yes	No	Yes
R^2	0.099	0.1157	0.1216	0.1533	0.0799	0.1049	0.054	0.0964	0.06	0.1479	0.0551	0.1235
N	15,436		6,872		8,564		5,976		2,503		3,473	

Note: **: P<0.01, *: P<0.05, †: P<0.1. Standard errors (reported in parentheses) are clustered by municipality of assignment in specification 1 and neighborhood of assignment in specification 2. Additional controls: age and age squared, indicators for marital status, having a child aged 0-2, having a child aged 3-17, educational attainment, year of immigration and country of origin and socioeconomic municipality characteristics (log(inhabitants), unemployment rate, log(average gross income), log(pct. non-Western immigrants) and log(pct. co-nationals)). Values of control variables are measured in the year of assignment. Share of individuals living in a socially deprived neighborhood (defined as a neighborhood in which at most 60% of individuals aged 18-60 are employed): 0.352.

Source: Administrative registers from Statistics Denmark.

Table 5: Geographical distribution across types of neighborhoods of the overall population in Denmark and subgroups of the population.

	Overall population in Denmark in 1991	Non-Western immigrants in 1991	Initial residence of refugee men in the balanced sample
	1	2	3
Neighborhood type:			
Socially deprived	3.9	22.8	16.7
Not socially deprived	96.1	77.2	83.3

Note: A socially deprived neighborhood is defined as a neighborhood in which at most 60% of individuals aged 18-60 are employed.

Source: Administrative register data from Statistics Denmark.

Table 6: Location assignment of male, non-Western refugees: Mean (standard deviation) of personal attributes in the year of assignment. Balanced panel of refugee men.

	Neighborhood of assignment:		t-test of difference in means
	Socially deprived	Non-deprived	
	1	2	3
Years of education:			
0-9 years	0.126	0.119	1.05
	(0.33)	(0.32)	
10-12 years	0.375	0.392	1.59
	(0.48)	(0.49)	
At least 13 years	0.169	0.165	0.42
	(0.37)	(0.37)	
Unknown education	0.330	0.324	0.57
	(0.47)	(0.47)	
Age	32.1	30.4	6.54
	(12.9)	(10.7)	
Marital status	0.523	0.467	5.15
	(0.50)	(0.50)	
Child aged 0-2	0.123	0.111	1.66
	(0.33)	(0.31)	
Child aged 3-17	0.231	0.179	5.84
	(0.42)	(0.38)	
N	2,573	12,863	

Source: Administrative register data from Statistics Denmark.

Table 7. OLS estimates. Dependent variable: Indicator for having moved out of the neighbourhood of assignment in year t+6. Balanced panel of male refugees.

	1	2	3	4	5	6	7
Educational attainment:							
0-9 years of education	Ref.	Ref.	Ref.	Ref.	Ref.	Ref.	Ref.
10-12 years of education	-0.003	-0.003	-0.004	-0.004	-0.002	-0.003	-0.003
	(0.012)	(0.011)	(0.011)	(0.011)	(0.011)	(0.012)	(0.011)
More than 12 years of education	0.000	-0.002	-0.003	-0.003	0.001	-0.001	-0.002
	(0.011)	(0.010)	(0.010)	(0.010)	(0.010)	(0.011)	(0.010)
Unknown education	-0.007	-0.004	-0.005	-0.005	-0.006	-0.006	-0.004
	(0.013)	(0.013)	(0.013)	(0.013)	(0.013)	(0.013)	(0.013)
Age	-0.004**	-0.004**	-0.004**	-0.004**	-0.004**	-0.004**	-0.004**
	(0.000)	(0.000)	(0.000)	(0.000)	(0.000)	(0.000)	(0.000)
Married	-0.008	-0.008	-0.008	-0.008	-0.008	-0.009	-0.007
	(0.009)	(0.008)	(0.008)	(0.008)	(0.009)	(0.008)	(0.008)
Having a child aged 0-2	-0.060**	-0.058**	-0.059**	-0.059**	-0.061**	-0.059**	-0.059**
	(0.012)	(0.011)	(0.011)	(0.011)	(0.012)	(0.012)	(0.011)
Having a child aged 3-17	-0.082**	-0.075**	-0.075**	-0.075**	-0.084**	-0.083**	-0.077**
	(0.015)	(0.015)	(0.015)	(0.014)	(0.015)	(0.015)	(0.014)
Neighborhood characteristics:							
Socially deprived neighborhood		-0.155**	-0.123**	-0.123**			-0.115**
		(0.020)	(0.021)	(0.021)			(0.021)
ln(pct. non-Western immigrant men aged 18-60)			-0.022**	-0.023**			-0.026**
			(0.006)	(0.006)			(0.006)
ln(pct. co-national men aged 18-60)				0.001			-0.002
				(0.004)			(0.005)
ln(employment rate of non-Western immigrant men aged 18-60)					-0.004*		-0.004†
					(0.002)		(0.002)
No other non-Western immigrant men aged 18-60					-0.117**		-0.126**
					(0.043)		(0.042)
ln(mployment rate of co-national men aged 18-60)						-0.006**	-0.004**
						(0.001)	(0.001)
No co-national men aged 18-60						0.012	-0.004
						(0.012)	(0.012)
R-squared	0.075	0.098	0.100	0.100	0.081	0.078	0.110
N				15,436			

Note: †: P<0.1, *: P<0.05, **: P<0.01. Standard errors (clustered by municipality of assignment) reported in parentheses. Additional controls: Indicators for year of immigration and country of origin and socioeconomic municipality characteristics (log(inhabitants), unemployment rate, log(average gross income), log(pct. non-Western immigrants) and log(pct. co-nationals)). Values of control variables are measured in the year of assignment.

Source: Administrative registers from Statistics Denmark.

Table 8: OLS and 2SLS estimates of the effect of living in a socially deprived neighborhood on individual labor market outcomes. Balanced panel of male refugees: YSM=2-6.

	Dependent variable:											
	Employed in Nov.						Log(real annual earnings)					
	All		Low-skilled		Highly skilled		All		Low-skilled		Highly skilled	
	1	2	3	4	5	6	7	8	9	10	11	12
Panel A: OLS estimates												
Current residence in a socially deprived neigborhood	-0.028**	-0.027**	-0.017**	-0.016**	-0.037**	-0.034**	-0.070*	-0.062*	-0.024	-0.011	-0.115**	-0.102**
	(0.003)	(0.003)	(0.004)	(0.004)	(0.005)	(0.005)	(0.029)	(0.028)	(0.034)	(0.034)	(0.038)	(0.038)
Panel B: Intent-to-treat estimates (OLS)												
Assigned to a socially deprived neigborhood	0.004	0.009	0.005	0.005	0.002	0.011	0.065	0.075	0.04	0.022	0.081	0.108*
	(0.008)	(0.005)	(0.012)	(0.012)	(0.008)	(0.006)	(0.043)	(0.040)	(0.060)	(0.063)	(0.042)	(0.046)
Panel C: 2SLS estimates												
Current residence in a socially deprived neighborhood	0.014	0.038	0.019	0.022	0.008	0.043	0.241	0.316	0.129	0.036	0.306	0.456
	(0.020)	(0.028)	(0.027)	(0.038)	(0.030)	(0.040)	(0.147)	(0.215)	(0.208)	(0.350)	(0.203)	(0.271)
First stage of 2SLS (OLS):												
Assignment to a socially deprived neighbourhood	0.297**	0.242**	0.311**	0.247**	0.286**	0.237**	0.274**	0.210**	0.274**	0.185**	0.277**	0.231**
	(0.026)	(0.024)	(0.026)	(0.026)	(0.027)	(0.025)	(0.029)	(0.026)	(0.035)	(0.036)	(0.033)	(0.029)
Controls for area of assignment:												
Socio-economic and demographic municipality characteristics	Yes	Yes	Yes	Yes	Yes	Yes	Yes	Yes	Yes	Yes	Yes	Yes
Municipality of assignment FE	No	Yes	No	Yes	No	Yes	No	Yes	No	Yes	No	Yes
Number of observations	77,180		34,360	42,820			24,725		10,595		14,130	
Number of individuals	15,436		6,872	8,564			8,864		3,849		5,015	

Note: **: P<0.01, *: P<0.05. Standard errors are reported in parentheses. Additional controls: individual random effect, age and age squared, indicators for marital status, having a child aged 0-2, having a child aged 3-17, educational attainment, YSM, year of immigration and country of origin and socioeconomic municipality characteristics (log(inhabitants), unemployment rate, log(average gross income), log(pct. non-Western immigrants) and log(pct. co-nationals)). Values of control variables are measured in the year of assignment. Share of individuals assigned to a socially deprived neighborhood (defined as a neighborhood in which at most 60% of individuals aged 18-60 are employed): 0.167
Source: Administrative registers from Statistics Denmark.

Table 9: OLS and 2SLS estimates of the effect of ln(employment rate of men aged 18-60 living in the neighbourhood of residence) on individual labour market outcomes. Balanced panel of male refugees: YSM=2-6.

	Dependent variable:							
	Employed in Nov.				Ln(real annual earnings)			
	All	Low-skilled		Highly skilled	All	Low-skilled		Highly
	1	2	3	4	5	6	7	8
Panel A: OLS estimates								
Ln(employment rate of men aged 18-60 living in current neighborhood of residence)	0.090** (0.009)	0.087** (0.008)	0.059** (0.009)	0.108** (0.011)	0.314** (0.082)	0.310** (0.075)	0.225** (0.072)	0.090* (0.024)
Panel B: Intent-to-treat estimates (OLS)								
Ln(employment rate of men aged 18-60 living in neighborhood of assignment)	-0.001 (0.016)	-0.002 (0.012)	-0.007 (0.026)	0.005 (0.013)	-0.135 (0.109)	-0.092 (0.102)	-0.108 (0.140)	-0.074 (0.103)
Panel C: 2SLS estimates								
Ln(employment rate of men aged 18-60 living in current neighborhood of residence)	-0.007 (0.036)	-0.007 (0.047)	-0.024 (0.064)	0.020 (0.068)	-0.469 (0.302)	-0.358 (0.420)	-0.334 (0.651)	-0.315 (0.545)
First stage of 2SLS:								
Ln(employment rate of men aged 18-60 living in neighbourhood of assignment)	0.370** (0.036)	0.309** (0.038)	0.323** (0.035)	0.298** (0.039)	0.301** (0.028)	0.236** (0.027)	0.221** (0.040)	0.247** (0.023)
Controls for area of assignment:								
Socio-economic and demographic municipality characteristics	Yes	Yes	Yes	Yes	Yes	Yes	Yes	Yes
Municipality of assignment FE	No	Yes	Yes	Yes	No	Yes	Yes	Yes
Number of observations	77,180	34,360	6,872	42,820	24,725	10,595	3,849	14,130
Number of individuals	15,436			8,564	8,864			5,015

Note: **: P<0.01, *: P<0.05. Standard errors are reported in parentheses. Additional controls: individual random effect, age and age squared, indicators for marital status, having a child aged 0-2, having a child aged 3-17, educational attainment, YSM, year of immigration and country of origin and socioeconomic municipality characteristics (log(inhabitants), unemployment rate, log(average gross income), log(pct. non-Western immigrants) and log(pct. co-nationals)). Values of control variables are measured in the year of assignment. Ln(employment rate of men aged 18-60 living in the neighbourhood of residence 2-6 years after immigration) has a mean (std. dev.) of 4.22 (0.234).
Source: Administrative registers from Statistics Denmark.

Table 10: OLS and 2SLS estimates of the effect of ln(employment rate of non-Western immigrant men aged 18-60 living in the neighborhood of residence) on individual labor market outcomes. Balanced panel of male refugees: YSM=2-6.

	Dependent variable:													
	Employed in Nov.							Ln(real annual earnings)						
	All		Low-skilled		Highly skilled		All		All		Low-skilled		Highly skilled		All
	1	2	3	4	5	6	7	8	9	10	11	12	13	14
Panel A: OLS estimates of characteristics of current neighborhood of residence														
Ln(employment rate of non-Western immigrant men aged 18-60)	0.010**	0.010**	0.009**	0.010**		0.011**	0.011**	0.054**	0.053**	0.058**	0.048**		0.054**	0.059**
	(0.002)	(0.002)	(0.002)	(0.002)		(0.002)	(0.002)	(0.010)	(0.011)	(0.013)	(0.013)		(0.011)	(0.011)
Ln(pct. non-Western immigrant men aged 18-60)		-0.014**	-0.014**	-0.033**		-0.014**	-0.033**		-0.039**	-0.042**	-0.126**		-0.039**	-0.042**	-0.126**
		(0.002)	(0.002)	(0.005)		(0.002)	(0.005)		(0.011)	(0.011)	(0.035)		(0.011)	(0.011)	(0.035)
Ln(employment rate of non-Western immigrant men aged 18-60)*ln(pct. non-Western immigrant men aged 18-60)							0.006**							0.025*
							(0.001)							(0.010)
Panel B: 2SLS estimates of characteristics of current neighborhood of residence														
Ln(employment rate of non-western immigrant men aged 18-60)	0.014	0.065†	0.048	0.086†		0.071†	0.075*	0.486*	0.808**	0.768	0.892*		0.815**	0.812**
	(0.029)	(0.039)	(0.060)	(0.048)		(0.039)	(0.035)	(0.243)	(0.295)	(0.488)	(0.374)		(0.296)	(0.249)
Ln(pct. non-Western immigrant men aged 18-60)		-0.023†	-0.025*	-0.129		-0.025*	-0.129		-0.081	-0.135	-0.708		-0.081	-0.135	-0.708
		(0.012)	(0.013)	(0.101)		(0.013)	(0.101)		(0.096)	(0.118)	(1.000)		(0.096)	(0.118)	(1.000)
Ln(employment rate of non-Westerm immig. men aged 18-60)*ln(pct. non-Western immig. men aged 18-60)							0.032							0.173
							(0.030)							(0.285)
First stage of 2SLS:														
Effects on ln(employment rate of non-Western immigrant men aged 18-60 living in current neighborhood of residence):														
Ln(employment rate of non-Western immigrant men aged 18-60 living in assigned neighborh.)	0.038**	0.031**	0.026**	0.039**		0.031**	0.031**	0.027**	0.028**	0.022*	0.033**		0.028**	0.028**
	(0.006)	(0.005)	(0.007)	(0.006)		(0.005)	(0.005)	(0.006)	(0.005)	(0.009)	(0.008)		(0.005)	(0.006)
No other non-Western immigrant men aged 18-60 in assigned neighborhood	-0.078†	-0.156**	-0.151**	-0.154**		-0.155**	-0.157**	-0.079	-0.166**	-0.164**	-0.143†		-0.163**	-0.163**
	(0.044)	(0.048)	(0.057)	(0.055)		(0.048)	(0.047)	(0.049)	(0.055)	(0.062)	(0.081)		(0.055)	(0.055)
Effects on ln(pct. non-Western immigrant men aged 18-60 living in neighborhood of residence):														
Ln(pct. non-Western immigrant men aged 18-60 in assigned neighborhood)		0.202**	0.202**	0.166**		0.202**	0.166**		0.164**	0.165**	0.124**		0.164**	0.165**	0.124**
		(0.024)	(0.024)	(0.021)		(0.024)	(0.021)		(0.018)	(0.018)	(0.017)		(0.018)	(0.018)	(0.017)
Effect on ln(employment rate of non-Western immigrant men in neighborhood):														
Ln(employment rate of non-Western immig. Men in assigned neighborhood)*ln(pct. non-Western immig. men in assigned neighborh.)							0.069**							0.072**
							(0.016)							(0.016)

Controls for area of assignment:											
Socio-economic and demographic municipality characteristics	Yes	Yes	Yes	Yes	Yes	Yes	Yes	Yes	Yes	Yes	Yes
Municipality of assignment FE	No	Yes	Yes	Yes	Yes	Yes	No	Yes	Yes	Yes	Yes
Number of observations	77,180		34,360	42,820		77,180	24,725	10,595	14,130		24,725
Number of individuals	15,436	6,872	8,564		15,436		8,864	3,849	5,015		8,864

Note: **: P<0.01, *: P<0.05, †: P<0.1. Standard errors are reported in parentheses. Additional controls: individual random effect, age and age squared, indicators for marital status, having a child aged 0-2, having a child aged 3-17, educational attainment, YSM, year of immigration and country of origin, municipality of assignment and socioeconomic municipality characteristics (log(inhabitants), unemployment rate, log(average gross income), log(pct. non-Western immigrants) and log(pct. co-nationals)). Values of control variables are measured in the year of assignment. Ln(employment rate of non-Western immigrant men aged 18-60 living in the neighborhood of residence 2-6 years after immigration) has a mean (std. dev.) of 3.47 (1.048) and ln(pct. non-Western immigrant men aged 18-60 living in the neighborhood of residence 2-6 years after immigration) has a mean (std. dev.) of 1.97 (1.19).

Source: Administrative registers from Statistics Denmark.

Table 11: OLS and 2SLS estimates of the effect of ln(employment rate of co-national men aged 18-60 living in the neighborhood of residence) on individual labor market outcomes. Balanced panel of male refugees: YSM=2-6.

	Dependent variable:													
	Employed in Nov.							Ln(real annual earnings)						
	All		Low-skilled		Highly skilled		All		All		Low-skilled		Highly skilled		All
	1	2	3	4	5	6	7	8	9	10	11	12	13	14

Panel A: OLS estimates of chacteristics of current neighborhood of residence

Ln(employment rate of co-national men aged 18-60)
| 0.009** | 0.008** | 0.007** | 0.009** | | 0.010** | 0.008** | 0.057** | 0.055** | 0.051** | 0.058** | | 0.059** | 0.055** |
| (0.001) | (0.001) | (0.001) | (0.001) | | (0.001) | (0.001) | (0.003) | (0.003) | (0.006) | (0.004) | | (0.003) | (0.003) |

Ln(pct. co-national men aged 18-60)
| | | | | -0.007** | -0.019** | | | | | | -0.015 | -0.059** | |
| | | | | (0.002) | (0.002) | | | | | | (0.010) | (0.009) | |

Ln(employment rate of non-Western immigrant men aged 18-60)
| | | | | | | 0.005** | | | | | | | 0.007 |
| | | | | | | (0.002) | | | | | | | (0.011) |

Panel A: 2SLS estimates of characteristics of current neighborhood of residence

Ln(employment rate of co-national men aged 18-60)
| 0.011 | 0.009 | 0.005 | 0.009 | | 0.007 | 0.007 | 0.437** | 0.407** | 0.316 | 0.289* | | 0.528* | 0.419* |
| (0.011) | (0.011) | (0.016) | (0.015) | | (0.015) | (0.013) | (0.150) | (0.154) | (0.232) | (0.144) | | (0.259) | (0.202) |

Ln(pct. co-national men aged 18-60) (2SLS)
| | | 0.012 | 0.003 | | | | | | 0.449† | -0.452 | |
| | | (0.021) | (0.027) | | | | | | (0.234) | (0.518) | |

Ln(employment rate of non-Western immigrant men aged 18-60)
| | | | | | | 0.022 | | | | | | | -0.006 |
| | | | | | | (0.044) | | | | | | | (0.510) |

First stage of 2SLS:

Effects on ln(employment rate of co-national men living in current neighborhood of residence):

Ln(employment rate of co-national men aged 18-60 living in assigned neighborhood)
| 0.030** | 0.028** | 0.021† | 0.035** | | 0.024** | 0.027** | 0.017† | 0.014 | 0.002 | 0.027* | | 0.011 | 0.001 |
| (0.007) | (0.007) | (0.011) | (0.010) | | (0.007) | (0.007) | (0.010) | (0.011) | (0.013) | (0.014) | | (0.012) | (0.004) |

No co-national men aged 18-60 in assigned neighborhood
| -0.424** | -0.451** | -0.481** | -0.431** | | -0.315** | -0.456** | -0.297** | -0.310** | -0.284* | -0.321** | | -0.198** | -0.081** |
| (0.073) | (0.068) | (0.081) | (0.081) | | (0.068) | (0.067) | (0.079) | (0.083) | (0.120) | (0.092) | | (0.090) | (0.030) |

Effects on instruments on ln(pct. co-national men living in current neighborhood of residence):

Ln(pct. co-national men aged 18-60 living in assigned neighborhood)
| | | 0.110** | 0.111** | | | | | | 0.067** | 0.068** | |
| | | (0.030) | (0.029) | | | | | | (0.019) | (0.018) | |

Effect on ln(employment rate of non-Western immigrant men aged 18-60 living in current neighborhood of residence):

Ln(employment rate of non-Western immig. men aged 18-60 living in assigned neighbourh.)
| | | | | | | 0.029** | | | | | | | 0.026** |
| | | | | | | (0.005) | | | | | | | (0.005) |

Controls for area of assignment:									
Socio-economic and demographic municipality characteristics	Yes	Yes	Yes	Yes	Yes	Yes	Yes	Yes	Yes
Municipality of assignment FE	No	Yes	Yes	Yes	Yes	No	Yes	Yes	Yes
Number of observations	77,180	77,180	34,360	42,820	77,180	24,725	10,595	14,130	24,725
Number of individuals	15,436	15,436	6,872	8,564	15,436	8,864	3,849	5,015	8,864

Note: **: $P<0.01$, *: $P<0.05$, †: $P<0.1$. Standard errors are reported in parentheses. Additional controls: individual random effect, age and age squared, indicators for marital status, having a child aged 0-2, having a child aged 3-17, educational attainment, YSM, year of immigration and country of origin and socioeconomic municipality characteristics (log(inhabitants), unemployment rate, log(average gross income), log(pct. non-Western immigrants) and log(pct. co-nationals)). Values of control variables are measured in the year of assignment. Ln(employment rate of co-national men aged 18-60 living in the neighborhood of residence 2-6 years after immigration) has a mean (std. dev.) of 0.68 (3.89), ln(pct. co-national men aged 18-60 living in neighborhood of residence 2-6 years after assignment) has a mean (std. dev.): 0.014 (1.37) and ln(employment rate of non-Western immigrant men aged 18-60 living in the neighborhood of residence 2-6 years after immigration) has a mean (std. dev.) of 3.47 (1.048).

Source: Administrative registers from Statistics Denmark.

Table 12: 2SLS estimates of characteristics of current neighborhood of residence on individual labor market outcomes. Balanced panel of male refugees: YSM=2-6. Refugees assigned to Copenhagen or Frederiksberg municipality are excluded.

	Dependent variable:													
	Employed in Nov.							Ln(real annual earnings)						
	1	2	3	4	5	6	7	8	9	10	11	12	13	14
Current neighborhood of residence:														
Socially deprived	0.025							0.348						
	(0.028)							(0.215)						
Ln(employment rate of men aged 18-60)		-0.007							-0.504					
		(0.048)							(0.415)					
Ln(employment rate of non-Western immigrant men aged 18-60)			0.100*	0.083*						0.828*	0.795***			
			(0.045)	(0.042)						(0.332)	(0.303)			
Ln(pct. non-Western immigrant men aged 18-60)				-0.022†							-0.090			
				(0.013)							(0.121)			
Ln(employment rate of co-national men aged 18-60)					0.010	0.007	0.003					0.343*	0.527*	0.452
					(0.012)	(0.015)	(0.015)					(0.139)	(0.258)	(0.280)
Ln(pct. co-national men aged 18-60)						0.003							-0.450	
						(0.027)							(0.518)	
Controls for area of assignment:														
Socio-economic and demographic municipality characteristics					Yes	Yes	Yes	Yes	Yes			Yes	Yes	Yes
Municipality of assignment FE			Yes	Yes	Yes	Yes	Yes	Yes	Yes	Yes	Yes	Yes	Yes	Yes
Number of observations	67,830							22,385						
Number of individuals	13,566							7,941						

Note: ***: P<0.01, *: P<0.05, †: P<0.1. Standard errors are reported in parentheses. Additional controls: individual random effect, age and age squared, indicators for marital status, having a child aged 0-2, having a child aged 3-17, educational attainment, YSM, year of immigration and country of origin and socioeconomic municipality characteristics (log(inhabitants), unemployment rate, log(average gross income), log(pct. non-Western immigrants) and log(pct. co-nationals)). Values of control variables are measured in the year of assignment. Ln(employment rate of men aged 18-60 living in the neighborhood of residence 2-6 years after immigration) has a mean (std. dev.) of 4.22 (0.234), ln(employment rate of non-Western immigrant men aged 18-60 living in the neighborhood of residence 2-6 years after immigration) has a mean (std. dev.) of 3.47 (1.048), ln(pct. non-Western immigrant men aged 18-60 living in the neighborhood of residence 2-6 years after immigration) has a mean (std. dev.) of 1.97 (1.19), ln(employment rate of co-national men aged 18-60 living in the neighborhood of residence 2-6 years after immigration) has a mean (std. dev.) of 0.68 (3.89) and ln(pct. co-national men aged 18-60 living in neighborhood of residence 2-6 years after immigration) has a mean (std. dev.): 0.014 (1.37).

Source: Administrative registers from Statistics Denmark.

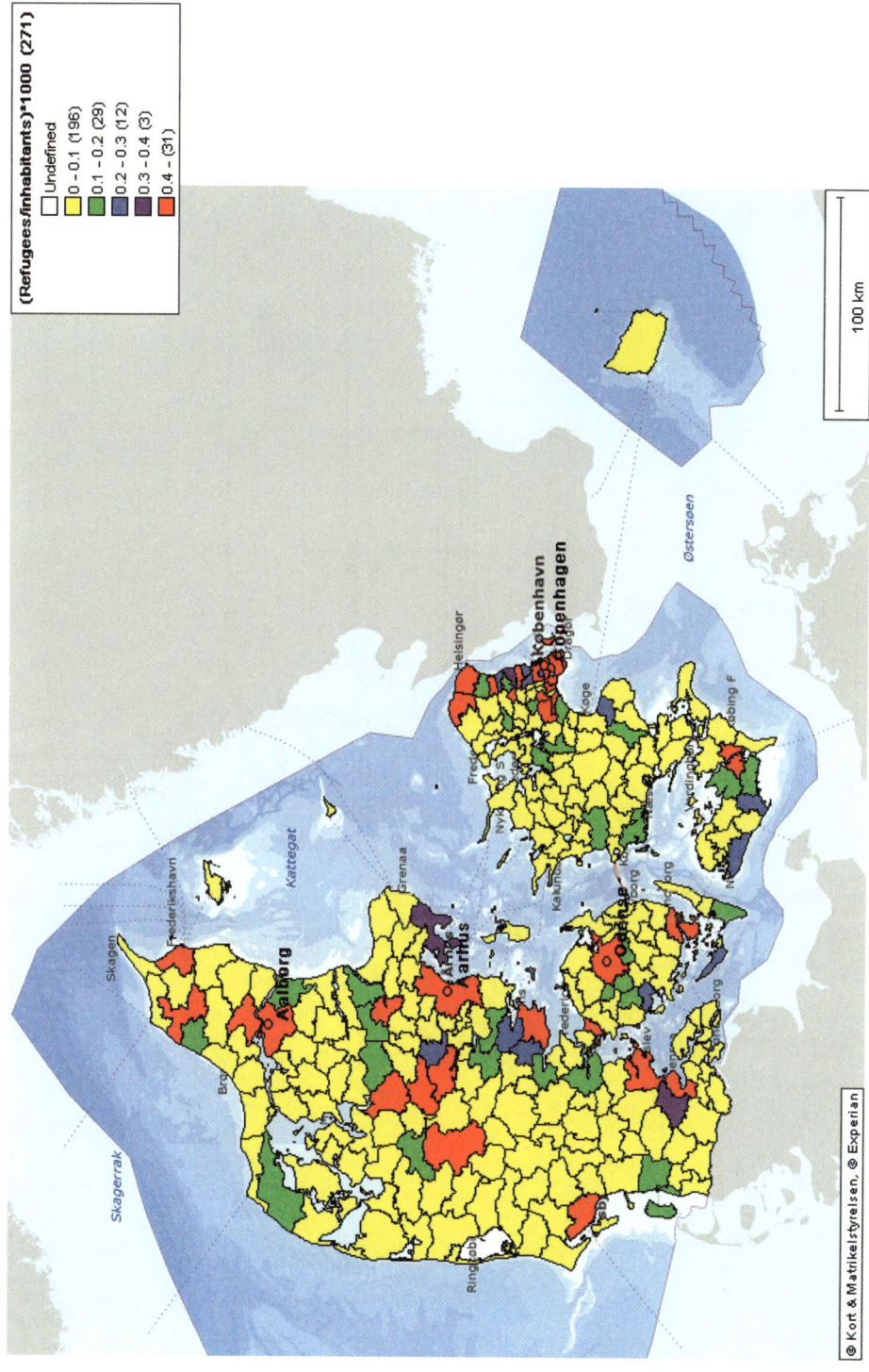

Fig. 1: Initial distribution of pre-reform refugees across municipalities (1980-1984).

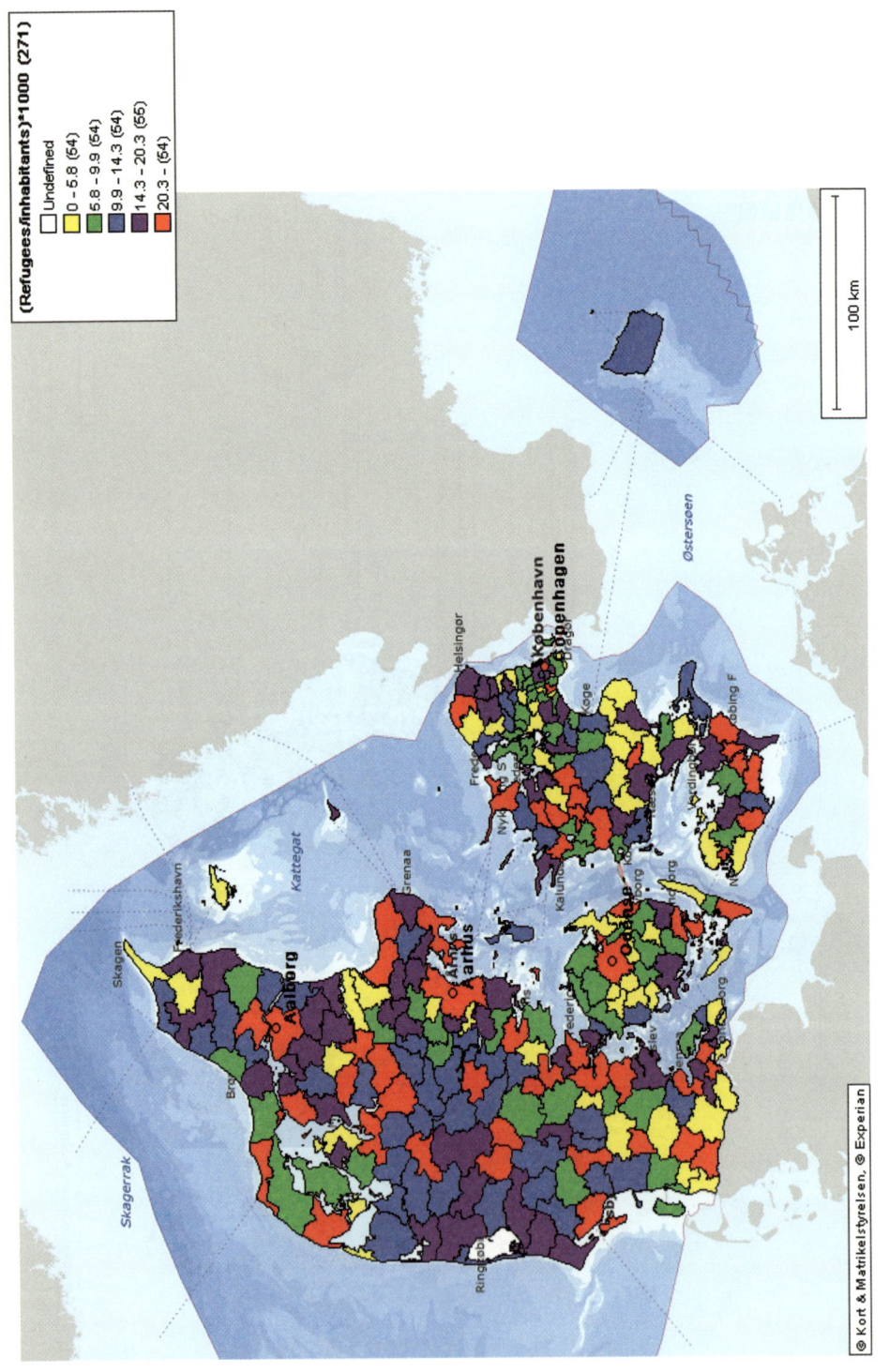

Fig. 2: Initial distribution of post-reform refugees across municipalities (1986-1998).

Table A1.A: Mean (standard deviation) of personal attributes and area characteristics in the year of assignment. Balanced sample of refugee men.

	All	Individuals assigned to	
		Socially deprived neighborhood	Non-deprived neighborhood
	1	2	3
Personal attributes:			
Age	30.65	32.13	30.35
	(11.14)	(12.89)	(10.73)
Married	0.476	0.523	0.467
	(0.500)	(0.500)	(0.499)
Having a child aged 0-2	0.113	0.123	0.111
	(0.317)	(0.328)	(0.314)
Having a child aged 3-17	0.188	0.231	0.179
	(0.390)	(0.422)	(0.383)
Educational attainment:			
0-9 years of education	0.12	0.126	0.119
	(0.325)	(0.332)	(0.324)
10-12 years of education	0.39	0.375	0.392
	(0.488)	(0.484)	(0.488)
More than 12 years of education	0.166	0.169	0.165
	(0.372)	(0.375)	(0.372)
Unknown education	0.325	0.33	0.324
	(0.469)	(0.470)	(0.468)
Year of immigration	1991	1992	1991
	(3.99)	(3.72)	(4.01)
Country of origin:			
Iran	0.151	0.134	0.155
	(0.358)	(0.341)	(0.362)
Iraq	0.237	0.286	0.227
	(0.425)	(0.452)	(0.419)
Vietnam	0.073	0.114	0.065
	(0.300)	(0.318)	(0.246)
Sri Lanka	0.135	0.046	0.155
	(0.342)	(0.208)	(0.362)
No citizenship	0.203	0.168	0.211
	(0.403)	(0.374)	(0.408)
Ethiopia	0.008	0.007	0.008
	(0.086)	(0.083)	(0.087)
Afghanistan	0.038	0.045	0.037
	(0.192)	(0.207)	(0.189)
Somalia	0.154	0.201	0.145
	(0.361)	(0.401)	(0.352)

Table A1.B: Mean (standard deviation) of personal attributes and area characteristics in the year of assignment. Balanced sample of refugee men.

	All	Individuals assigned to	
		Socially deprived neighborhood	Non-deprived neighborhood
	1	2	3
Neighborhood characteristics:			
Socially deprived neighborhood	0.167	1	0
	(0.361)		
Employment rate of men aged 18-60	76.12	53.76	80.59
	(13.13)	(8.40)	(8.53)
Employment rate of non-Western immigrant men aged 18-60	37.40	27.98	39.28
	(23.67)	(10.89)	(25.05)
Pct. non-Western immigrant men aged 18-60	6.93	21.23	4.08
	(9.05)	(12.00)	(4.51)
Employment rate of co-national men aged 18-60	15.98	16.98	15.78
	(26.34)	(20.48)	(27.36)
Pct. co-national men aged 18-60	0.92	2.81	0.54
	(1.72)	(2.98)	(0.96)
Municipality characteristics:			
Ln(inhabitants)	10.89	11.83	10.70
	(1.31)	(0.89)	(1.30)
Unemployment rate	9.85	11.22	9.58
	(2.97)	(2.45)	(2.99)
Ln(average gross income)	12.18	12.16	12.18
	(0.09)	(0.06)	(0.10)
Pct. non-Western immigrants	3.19	4.57	2.92
	(2.57)	(2.66)	(2.46)
Pct. co-nationals	0.18	0.28	0.16
	(0.20)	(0.22)	(0.20)
Housing characteristics:			
Private rental	0.417	0.122	0.456
	(0.493)	(0.327)	(0.500)
Public rental	0.328	0.814	0.231
	(0.470)	(0.389)	(0.422)
Unknown rental type	0.255	0.064	0.293
	(0.436)	(0.244)	(0.455)
One-family house	0.179	0.003	0.215
	(0.384)	(0.056)	(0.411)
Row house	0.071	0.04	0.077
	(0.256)	(0.195)	(0.266)
Apartment	0.492	0.876	0.415
	(0.500)	(0.329)	(0.493)
Dormitory	0.032	0.052	0.027
	(0.175)	(0.222)	(0.163)
Other housing type	0.021	0	0.025
	(0.142)		(0.156)
N	15,436	2,573	12,863

Source: Administrative register data from Statistics Denmark.

Table A2: Location assignment of individuals in balanced sample of refugee men.

Dependent variable: Neighborhood of assignment characteristics

	Socially deprived	Ln(employment rate of men)	Ln(employment rate of non-Western immigrant men)	Ln(pct. non-Western immigrant men)	Ln(employ-ment rate of co-national men)	Ln(pct. co-national men)
	1	2	3	4	5	6
Personal attributes in year t:						
Years of education (ref. cat.: 0-9 years):						
10-12 years	0.001	-0.001	-0.006	-0.006	-0.022	0.024
	(0.010)	(0.006)	(0.058)	(0.041)	(0.130)	(0.051)
More than 12 years	-0.015	0.01	-0.015	-0.097	-0.15	-0.069
	(0.012)	(0.009)	(0.072)	(0.060)	(0.206)	(0.067)
Age	0.0006	-0.0004	0.002	0.005**	0.021**	0.009**
	(0.0004)	(0.0002)	(0.002)	(0.002)	(0.004)	(0.002)
Married	0.001	-0.0004	0.034	-0.003	-0.155	-0.001
	(0.011)	(0.005)	(0.045)	(0.041)	(0.110)	(0.051)
Child aged 0-2	0.004	0.007	-0.09	-0.139**	0.1	-0.112
	(0.011)	(0.005)	(0.075)	(0.048)	(0.129)	(0.063)
Child aged 3-17	0.026**	-0.003	-0.049	-0.053*	-0.348*	-0.094
	(0.010)	(0.009)	(0.048)	(0.071)	(0.148)	(0.078)
R^2	0.035	0.106	0.03	0.1245	0.092	0.237
N				15,436		

Note: **: P<0.01, *: P<0.05. Standard errors are reported in parentheses. Additional controls: Dummies for country of origin, year of immigration and missing information about educational attainment.
Source: Administrative register data from Statistics Denmark.

Table A3: Share of individuals who have moved out of the neighborhood of assignment and municipality of assignment. Balanced sample of refugee men.

	Moved out of:	
	Assigned neighborhood	Assigned municipality
	1	2
Years since immigration:		
1	0	0
2	0.645	0.334
3	0.765	0.403
4	0.813	0.448
5	0.838	0.477
6	0.856	0.501
N	15,436	

Source: Administrative register data from Statistics Denmark.

Table A4: Mean (standard deviation) of dependent variables by years since migration (YSM). Balanced sample of refugee men.

	Dependent variable:						
	Employed in Nov.			Ln(real annual earnings)			
	All	Neighborhood of assignment:		All	Neighborhood of assignment:		
		Socially deprived	Non-deprived		Socially deprived	Non-deprived	
	1	2	3	4	5	6	
YSM=1	0.049	0.036	0.051	9.64	9.48	9.66	
	(0.215)	(0.187)	(0.22)	(1.7)	(1.81)	(1.68)	
N	15,436	2,573	12,863	1,556	197	1,359	
YSM=2	0.121	0.091	0.127	10.36	10.21	10.38	
	(0.326)	(0.288)	(0.333)	(1.54)	(1.63)	(1.53)	
N	15,436	2,573	12,863	3,321	412	2,909	
YSM=3	0.19	0.158	0.197	10.66	10.47	10.69	
	(0.393)	(0.365)	(0.398)	(1.53)	(1.61)	(1.52)	
N	15 436	2,573	12,863	4,605	638	3,967	
YSM=4	0.239	0.207	0.245	10.85	10.8	10.85	
	(0.427)	(0.405)	(0.43)	(1.51)	(1.55)	(1.51)	
N	15,436	2,573	12,863	5,177	717	4,460	
YSM=5	0.274	0.259	0.277	10.93	10.91	10.93	
	(0.446)	(0.438)	(0.447)	(1.50)	(1.62)	(1.48)	
N	15,436	2,573	12,863	5,646	821	4,825	
YSM=6	0.306	0.288	0.31	11.04	11	11.05	
	(0.461)	(0.453)	(0.463)	(1.46)	(1.50)	(1.45)	
N	15,436	2,573	12,863	5,976	889	5,087	

Note: Annual earnings are deflated using the consumer price index with base year 2000. For comparison, in 2000 84% of men aged 20-59 in Denmark was employed (www.Statistikbanken.dk/RASA and www.Statistikbanken.dk/BEF5) and the average annual earnings of male workers in Denmark were DKK 238,294 (www.Statistikbanken.dk/INDKP1).

Source: Administrative register data from Statistics Denmark.

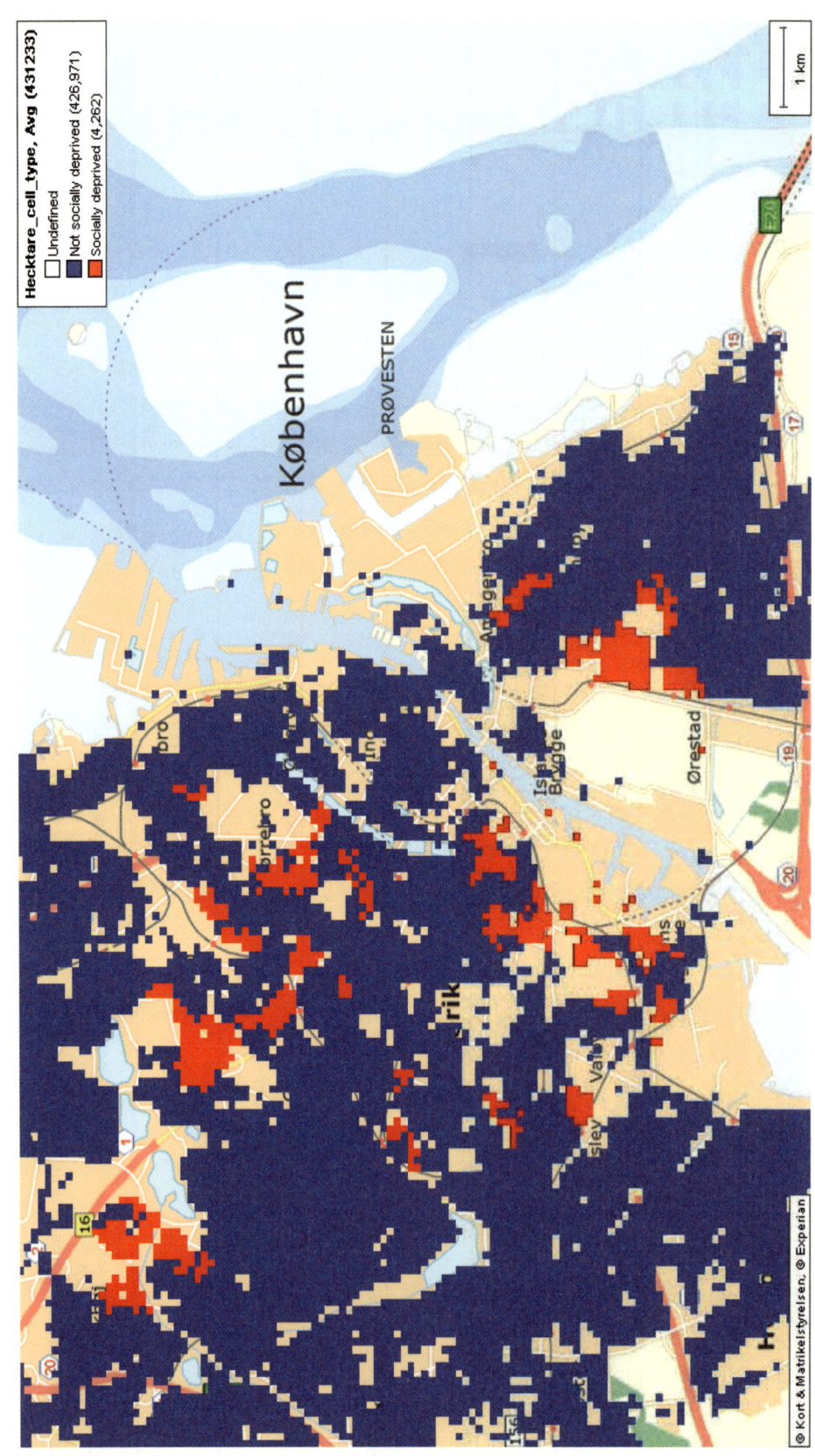

Fig. A1: Copenhagen.

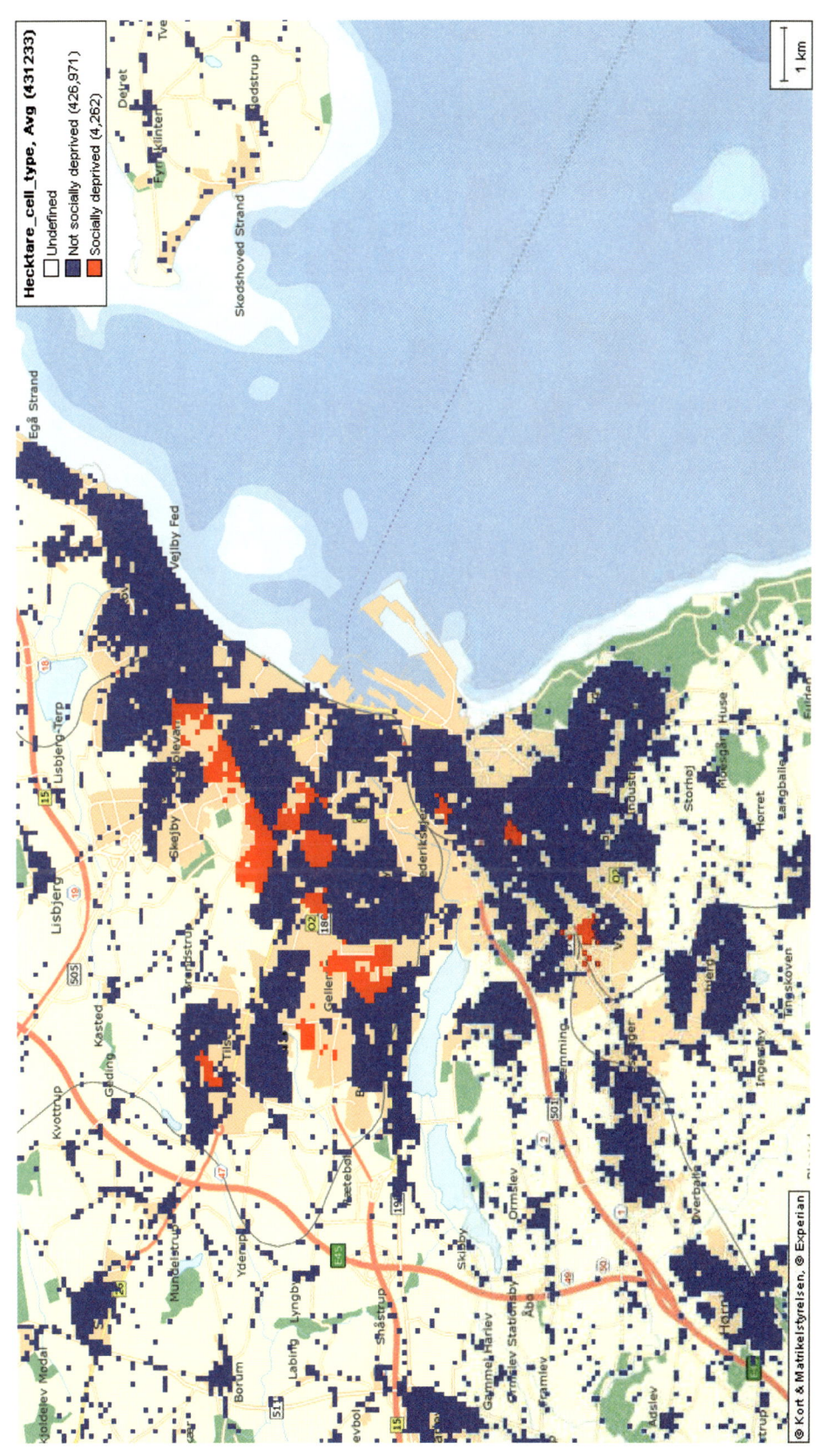

Fig. A2: Aarhus.

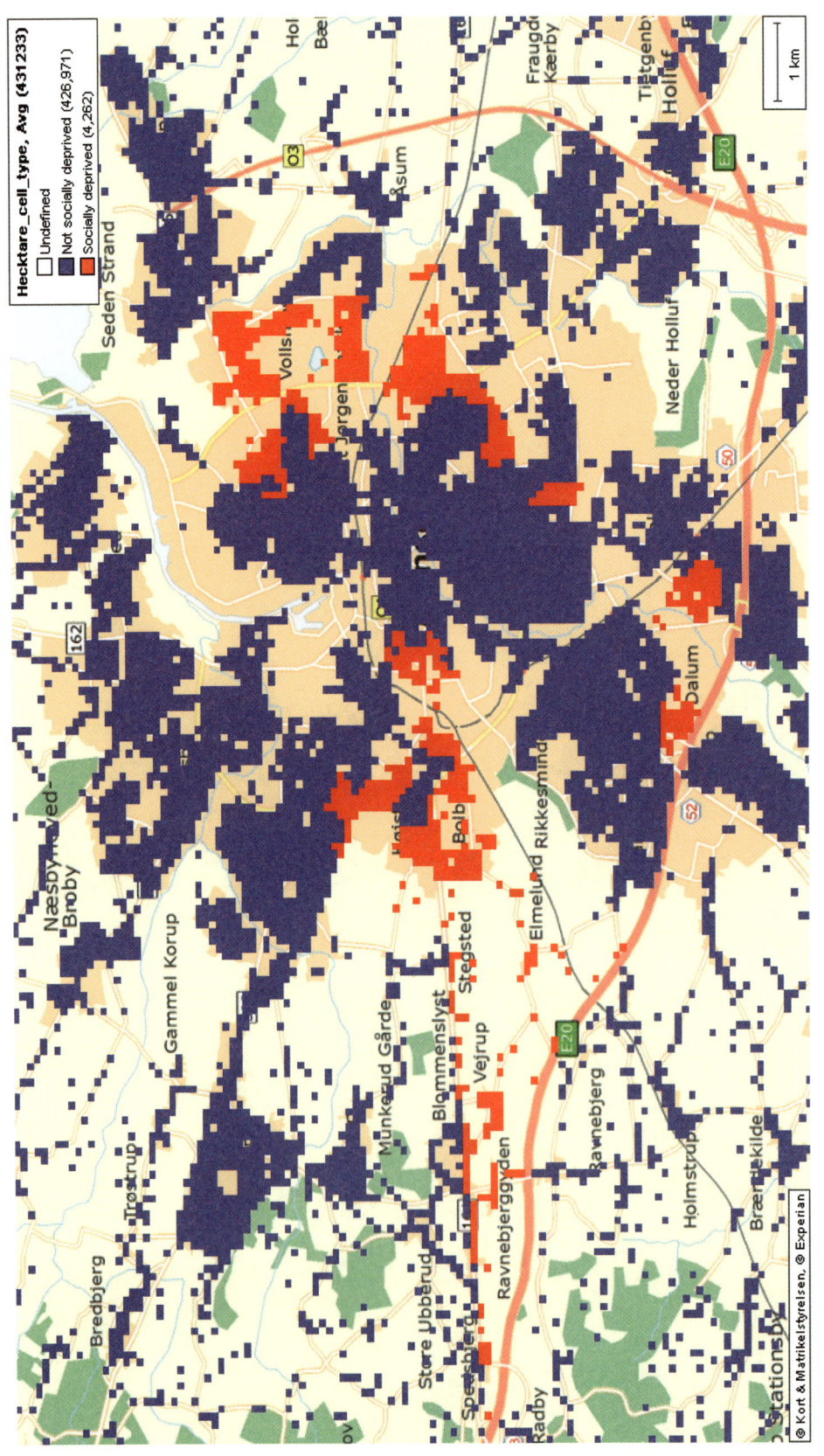

Fig. A3: Odense.

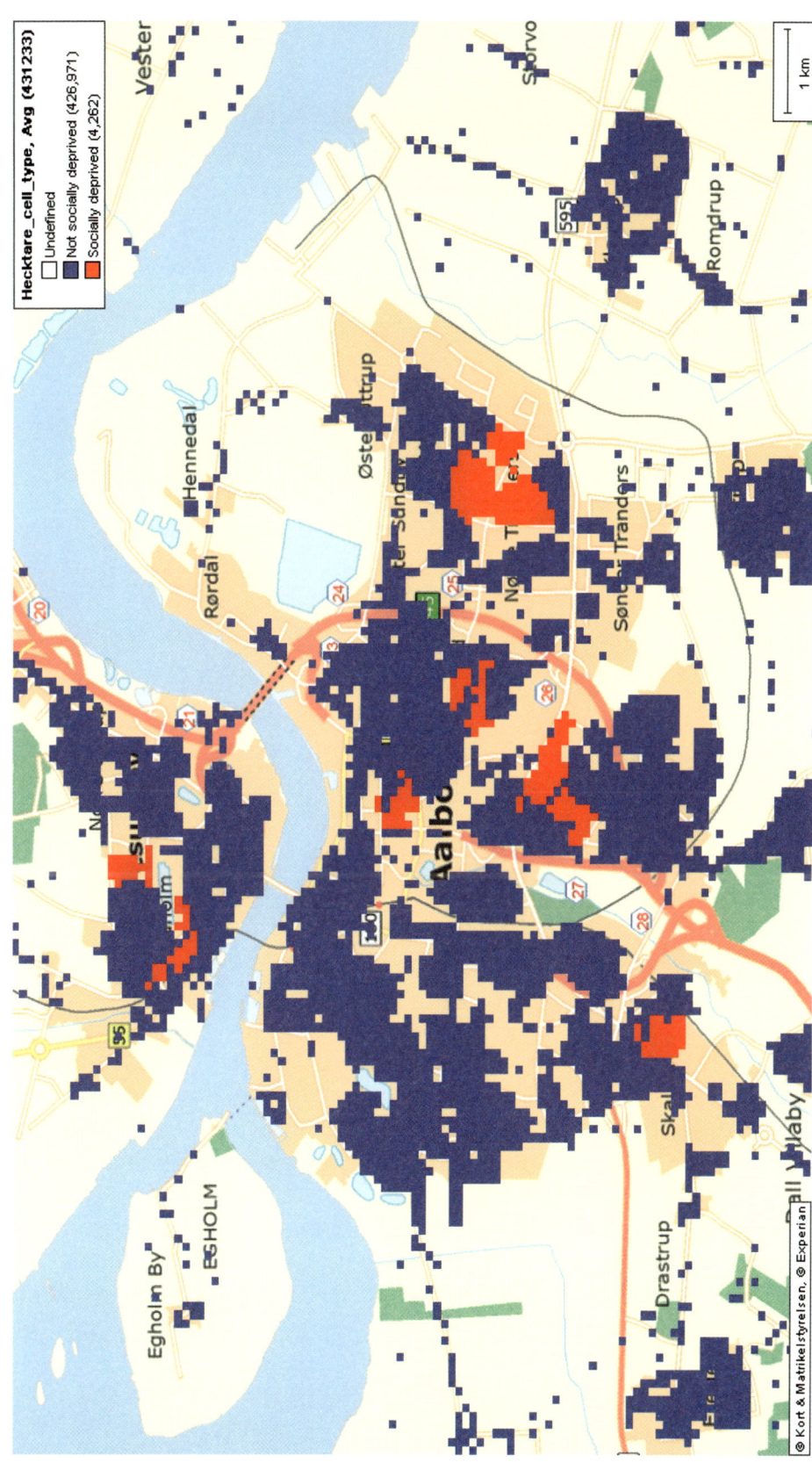

Fig. A4: Aalborg.